Too
Amazing
for Coincidence

Guided by
His Hand

Too
Amazing
for Coincidence

True Stories of
God's Mysterious Ways

Guided by
His Hand

EDITORS OF GUIDEPOSTS

Guideposts

A Gift from Guideposts

Thank you for your purchase! We want to express our gratitude for your support with a special gift just for you.

Dive into *Spirit Lifters*, a complimentary e-book that will fortify your faith, offering solace during challenging moments. Its 31 carefully selected scripture verses will soothe and uplift your soul.

Please use the QR code or go to **guideposts.org/ spiritlifters** to download.

Too Amazing for Coincidence: Guided by His Hand

Published by Guideposts
100 Reserve Road, Suite E200
Danbury, CT 06810
Guideposts.org

Cover and interior design by Judy Ross Graphic Design
Cover photo YOTUYA/iStock
Typeset by Aptara, Inc.

ISBN 978-1-961442-52-8 (hardcover)
ISBN 978-1-961442-53-5 (softcover)
ISBN 978-1-961442-54-2 (epub)

Printed and bound in the United States of America
10 9 8 7 6 5 4 3 2 1

Contents

A Well-Timed Phone Call

Sandy Kirby Quandt

If you say, "The LORD is my refuge," and you make the Most High your dwelling, no harm will overtake you, no disaster will come near your tent.

—PSALM 91:9–10 (NIV)

Magic Cookie Bars are a family favorite. It's a recipe I've made for years, especially around the holidays. On one particular day, however, I decided to make the dessert for no specific reason. No holiday. No celebration. No special event. I made it just because.

I pulled out the worn recipe and began to gather the ingredients. A stick of butter. Gluten-free graham cracker crumbs. Condensed milk. Semi-sweet chocolate chips. Shredded coconut. Usually, I melt the butter in a metal baking dish on the stovetop. But this time, for whatever reason, I decided to melt the butter in a glass baking dish instead. It wouldn't take long for me to learn how foolish that decision was.

I placed the stick of butter in the glass dish and turned on the burner, swirling the butter around as I waited for it to melt. Just before the butter melted completely, the phone on the wall across the room rang. I swirled the butter one last time, then went to answer the call.

"Hello?"

"Hi, Mom." My son, who wasn't in the habit of calling often, was on the line.

"What's up? Everything OK?"

"Yeah. Just thought I'd call. What're you doing?"

"Making Magic Cookie Bars."

"Yum. What's the occasion?"

"No occasion. Just thought I'd make them."

"I'll come over later. Save me some."

At that moment, the baking dish exploded with a loud, glass-shattering crack. Not more than six feet behind me, sizzling, hot, melted butter, and fragments of glass flew from the stovetop. Evidence of my ill-conceived butter melting method was everywhere. Globs of butter and shards of glass covered the floor, stovetop, and counter where I stood mere minutes earlier.

Alarm filled my son's voice. "What was that?"

It took a few seconds before I recovered from the surprise enough to answer. "I was melting butter in a glass baking dish on the stove. Not the smartest thing I've ever done. The dish exploded. Glass and butter are all over the kitchen."

"Are you OK?"

"Yeah. Just a little shaken. If you hadn't called when you did, I'd still be standing in front of the stove. The dish would have exploded right in my face, and I'd be picking glass out of my face and arms and dealing with burns. Don't want to think about what could have happened if it got into my eyes."

"That's pretty scary."

"Yeah."

"I'm glad you're OK."

"Me too. From now on, no more melting butter in a glass dish on the stovetop. I'm using the microwave."

"Sounds like a smart idea."

My son didn't call for any particular reason that day. He just felt like calling. Nothing special. Or so it seemed. The well-timed call caused me to step away from the stove, and that prevented me from being injured.

Was it a coincidence that my son happened to call me at the precise moment the baking dish exploded? I don't believe so. The timing was too perfect to be random. One second later, and I would have been seriously hurt. And being injured and alone in the house at the time would have presented its own set of challenges. There is no mistaking the fact God protected me.

As I cleaned up fragments of broken glass and globs of melted butter, I thanked God for His abiding presence, a presence that protected me from a dangerous situation and kept me from serious harm.

Over the years, when my son and I talk about the day the dish exploded, we never forget to marvel at how God used my son's phone call to draw me away from the stove at just the right moment.

I know God is always with me. Sometimes, though, I take His constant presence for granted. There are many times in my life where God's shield of protection kept me from being harmed, perhaps even without me realizing how close I had come. Now, whenever I pull out the butter-stained recipe card, gather the ingredients, and melt the butter in the microwave, I remember God's watchful protection—not just in that moment, but throughout my life.

Just as there was no specific reason for my son to call, there was no specific reason for me to make the Magic Cookie Bars. I simply made them just because. And that seemingly small choice provided a reminder that God's love and care never cease. His protection is constant. Just because.

Amazing Grace for the Journey

Jerry Brian Riess, as told to Wendy Lynne Smith

*Therefore we will not fear, though the earth give
way . . . though its waters roar and foam and
the mountains quake with their surging.*

—PSALM 46:2–3 (NIV)

I cringed inwardly as the rain pounded on the metal roof of the van, making deafening pinging sounds as the storm raged on. But our driver's hands stayed steady on the wheel and the newly installed tires on the van whirred smoothly on the narrow concrete road, allowing us to travel at highway speed despite the weather.

Suddenly, the van sputtered and lost all power.

"Are we out of gas?" I asked. It seemed unlikely. Our small group—Dean, who was driving the van; Dennis; and me as group leader—organized the distribution of food, clothing, and medicines at various churches and orphanages throughout this Eastern European region. We had prepared well for this journey. Our goal was to share the abiding love of our Heavenly Father with those far and near.

"No, we should have had enough," called Dean, affirming my thoughts.

What's going on, Lord? I prayed as our driver steered the van off the road. *I know You are guiding our journey, but I don't understand.*

When we had coasted to a complete halt, Dean turned the key again. The gauges lit up, allowing us to confirm that the gas tank was over half full, but the engine didn't start. As dusk began to darken the sky, all we could see was the blind curve ahead and the roadside picnic table adjacent to our vehicle.

"It could be dangerous to overnight here," commented Dennis as we discussed what to do. "This place is pretty far from the nearest town."

"Yeah, but it's going to be too dark to see soon. We can't work on the engine now," Dean countered.

After a short discussion, we determined that we would need to spend the night on the side of the road in our old, broken-down van. At least it seemed that God, in His infinite wisdom, had prepared a place for us to stop.

After a quick walk to stretch our legs, we climbed back into the damp van to wait out the night. Using duffel bags as pillows, we curled up in our sleeping bags and got as comfortable as we could. Because we had risen early that morning, and the drive had been tense because of the weather, the others were soon asleep.

But I lay awake for a long time listening to the sounds of the night, the splattering rain, and the occasional rumble of thunder. My mind wandered back over the events of the previous days, and the soothing melody of "Amazing Grace," which we had sung with a group of children after passing out clothes and toys. Recalling how the words of the song encourage complete trust and surrender in God's saving power, it became my prayer for divine protection that night. Shifting to get comfortable, I peered out the window at the inky black sky. Though I couldn't see anything, I sensed a continued presence of peace.

The rain had gone by morning, but we were now hemmed in by a heavy fog. I grabbed a flashlight out of the emergency kit, pulled my coat on, and stepped outside. Dean reluctantly followed me into the murky outdoors.

The road just ahead was completely underwater. Churning brown waves rushed over the pavement and spilled onto the dirt on each side, creating a muddy marsh.

"I hope we can fix the problem quickly," I said optimistically. I raised the hood to check the engine, cutting the dense haze with a beam of light. Though Dean and I checked all the connections, cables, and battery, we could see nothing wrong.

"Well, since there's nothing to repair, I'll try starting it," Dean said. He trotted around to the driver's side and climbed in. The engine rumbled to life. Exclamations of gratitude filled the air as we all found our seats.

Thank You, God, for a morning miracle! I prayed as we pulled onto the roadway and continued our journey. We drove around the hairpin curve, and I focused my mind on our day ahead. Soon, we would reach the church where I would speak.

I was so busy mentally rehearsing the message that God had put on my heart that I didn't notice that our van had stopped again just a short way from where we'd spent the night.

"Would you look at that!" Dean called. He was outside the van staring at something.

I scrambled out, and a whisp of fog swirled around me as I joined my friends in front of the vehicle.

"Whoa!" I gasped. The road just ahead was completely underwater. Churning brown waves rushed over the pavement and spilled onto the dirt on each side, creating a muddy marsh.

If our van had not mysteriously stopped before we reached the washed-out road, we would have driven straight into the flash flood and hydroplaned into the nearby ravine, drowning in the darkness. Together, we gazed at the dangerous, rushing waters. Surely God's guiding hand had protected us by divine intervention, and He had granted His peaceful presence through the long night.

I lifted my hands heavenward in a humble expression of praise and began to hum "Amazing Grace." The others joined in. With a grateful heart, I thanked God.

Soon, we continued on our way, reaching our destination by another route. But God's amazing grace and His hand of protection on our journey traveled with us everywhere we went.

The Green Rabbit and Amtrak

Laura Lee Leathers

Fear not, for I am with you; be not dismayed, for
I am your God; I will strengthen you, I will help you,
I will uphold you with my righteous right hand.

—ISAIAH 41:10 (ESV)

After completing our military service, my husband and I returned to Arkansas to his family's farm, where we planned to work in their farming operation. However, plans changed when my father-in-law had an opportunity to purchase cultivatable land in central Mississippi. Since we had not "settled," we were asked to move there to oversee the operation.

Farming was difficult in the late seventies because the cost of equipment was high and the crop prices had dropped, so our first crop with the family operation was trying. Arkansas had a drought, and the land barely produced a soybean crop. In Mississippi, the crop was good and balanced out the financial loss of the new Arkansas operation. The family made changes for the next crop year, and the harvest yields improved.

At the time, we owned a used two-door, grass-green Volkswagen Rabbit. We purchased the vehicle because we had owned a Volkswagen Beetle when we lived in Germany. It was a great vehicle, and that little car had no trouble keeping up with the Mercedes on the German Autobahn, a no-speed-limit highway. We certainly didn't have that high-speed luxury here. There were two big negatives to our car—there was no air conditioner, and the gear shift was on the floorboard, requiring extra effort to shift.

During this season, we lived in an old house on the property my father-in-law owned, which had some railroad tracks running through it. The tracks were very close to the house, sixty yards or less. The railroad built the line up on what might be called a levee, with overgrown brush and trees along the ditches on each side of the tracks.

Every morning, usually before ten o'clock, we knew there would be a southbound Amtrak train to Jackson. In the early evening, Amtrak headed northbound to Chicago. Between those were the freight trains. We learned their schedule, and we were always cautious around the times when those trains would be passing by, double-checking when crossing the tracks. From the house, we had a walking path to cross the tracks to get to the mailbox on the state highway, but the farm equipment and other vehicles had to drive down the country lane, climb a slight incline, and then cross. There were no railroad signs or signals. Our family members and visitors knew they were to look, listen, look again, and cautiously proceed.

One spring morning, before my husband left early to plant cotton, I reminded him that our toddler son and I would bring him lunch around noon. We would have a picnic under a tree near the field. After he departed, I started my morning routine and prepared our lunch.

Around 11:00 a.m., I placed my son in the back seat of the Rabbit (no car seats back in those days). After setting the food and canteen full of liquid on the floorboard in the front passenger side, I got into the driver's seat and drove down the gravel country lane. The Rabbit slowly climbed the incline to the railroad tracks. I stopped and rolled down the driver's side window to listen. I looked to my right and then to my left. Nothing. I looked again to the right, then left. Nothing.

I looked to my right, and coming out of the trees and into the clearing was the morning Amtrak train, late.

I pressed the gas pedal to start crossing the tracks slowly. Suddenly, a sound broke the silence—the Amtrak whistle. I looked to my right, and coming out of the trees and into the clearing was the morning Amtrak train, late. Even to this day, I remember seeing the headlight and the engineer's cab. The whistle blew again, but the train didn't slow down.

Fear gripped my heart.

I only had seconds to consider my options—life or death. I knew if I didn't do something quickly, the train would hit the front of the Rabbit, dragging us down the track or under the train.

Rather than pressing the accelerator to cross the track, I somehow managed to find the gear shift. I had to push the shift lock button that would allow me to put it in reverse. With my foot on the gas pedal, I backed up and off the tracks. Amtrak passed. My son and I were safe. Tears flowed.

I could never have moved fast enough to save us without God's intervention. Getting that old car in gear, traveling backward in time to avoid a train barreling at full speed toward us, just yards away—it shouldn't have been possible.

Some forty-plus years later, as I think about that situation, tears still come to my eyes. In God's graciousness and sovereignty, I know He helped me make the right choices, guiding my hand and sparing our lives.

Later I would wonder why I didn't hear the train earlier. It could have been how the sound waves travel through the terrain or the direction of the wind. Perhaps the engineer never blew the whistle until he saw me. I have no explanation.

What could have been a disaster settled down to become another peaceful day on the farm. The three of us enjoyed a picnic under the tree next to the cotton field with overwhelming gratitude, feeling God's grace spread over us.

GOD'S MYSTERIOUS MOMENTS: SAVED AT THE LAST MINUTE

Most of us won't see dramatic moments of danger like our writers did. But their stories remind us that God sees us in every moment of our lives. From a phone call putting us out of harm's way from a shattered glass dish to a stalled van keeping us from driving into a river, those things we don't expect show us God's constant care over us.

✵ **Pray.** Start every day by acknowledging God's protection over your life. Thank Him for His care. Communication with your heavenly Father throughout your day will help you remember that He's got all things in His hands.

✵ **Seek.** When delays in your schedule happen, remember it might just be God's hand holding you back from tragedy or putting you in the right place at the right time to help someone else.

✵ **Act.** Intentionally put every minute of your day in God's hands. Every time you get in a car, ask for His protection. When you're in traffic that's frustrating, acknowledge His sovereignty. Remember Mordecai's words to Esther: "And who knows whether you have not come to the kingdom for such a time as this?"

✵ **Reflect.** What would it look like if, instead of getting frustrated when your plans aren't going the way you want, you asked God to help you release your plans into His hands? As we've read in our stories today, God's timing, those annoying delays, can turn into amazing miracles.

Divine Vanity

Jeanne Roberson

───────────────

However, when He, the Spirit of truth, has come, He will guide you into all truth; for He will not speak on His own authority, but whatever He hears He will speak; and He will tell you things to come.

—JOHN 16:13 (NKJV)

I always said I would age gracefully and never nip or tuck anything. Then I reached my late fifties and noticed puffy pockets under my eyes. My lids had become heavy and drooped. I felt tired all the time. I tried chamomile tea bags, cucumbers, and all the recommended remedies, but nothing seemed to help.

For several months, I struggled with whether God viewed my desire to look better as an example of sinful vanity. I tried to push the thought away, but it returned every time I looked in the mirror. Ultimately, I surrendered to vanity and made an appointment with an ophthalmologist to have my eyelids reduced.

The doctor tested my vision from all angles. He agreed that removing the fatty tissue on my eyelids would improve my vision and that I'd feel much better. To my delight, insurance covered the procedure.

"I require a blood test before surgery," he explained. "Occasionally, thyroid and kidney disease are associated with these symptoms. There is nothing to worry about. The test is routine, and you will most likely be fine."

Elated at the idea that I would soon look and feel better, I went straight to the hospital and had my blood drawn.

A few days later, I received a phone call. My blood work had come back with an elevated white cell count—an indication something was wrong. Surgery had to be canceled.

The test results were devastating: there was a mass the size of a golf ball on my right kidney—possibly cancerous.

Filled with uncertainty, I immediately made an appointment with my primary care physician, praying it wasn't anything serious.

During our visit, my doctor recalled a minor urinary tract infection he had treated me for a few months prior. At the time, slight traces of blood were detected in my urine. After several days on an antibiotic, hints of blood were still visible, but I had no other symptoms. My doctor had assured me blood in the urine was not uncommon at my age. Feeling confident with his prognosis, I didn't give it another thought until the eye doctor called to cancel my surgery. Now we both wondered if it had been a symptom of something more serious.

I left my primary care physician's office with an order for a CAT scan, a referral to a urologist, and a heavy sinking feeling.

The urologist performed more tests, and the results were devastating: there was a mass the size of a golf ball on my right kidney—possibly cancerous.

The weeks that followed were filled with stressful doctor appointments and more tests. A surgeon at Brigham and Women's Hospital determined the mass was cancerous and needed to be removed immediately.

The moment I heard the word *cancer*, I became numb and lost all comprehension as my mind struggled to accept the unacceptable. I had to ask the doctor to repeat himself several times as he instructed me on what to expect next. Someone had to help me find my way out of the hospital. I drove home in a foggy state of shock.

The morning of Good Friday, I entered the hospital surrounded by my family. While the nurses prepped me for the operating room, I relinquished all my fears to God. My salvation was intact, and the outcome, whatever it may be, was in His hands. Nine hours later, laparoscopic surgery took a large portion of my right kidney. Pathology reports confirmed it was cancer, but the doctors concluded there was no indication it had spread.

After surgery, I was given a 95 percent cancer-free diagnosis. Radiation and chemotherapy were not necessary. Follow-up CAT scans would be vital for the next two years.

After all was said and done, I returned to the ophthalmologist to have my eyelids reduced. The doctor was thrilled to learn he had probably saved my life.

I hoped my cancer journey was over, at least the toughest parts. But when I went in for my six-month CAT scan, the oncologist reported an area of concern on my left lung. He ordered a PET scan to determine the cause.

The results came back, and again I had to process those words: "We think you have cancer."

"What type of cancer?"

"It could be related to renal cancer or lung cancer. Your three-month scan didn't show any areas of concern. The tumor board has concluded that due to the accelerated growth of the mass, you'll need immediate surgery. I'm sorry," he added.

A friend accompanied me to meet the recommended surgeon. We were brought to an examination room and waited for what seemed like hours. The doctor entered and spun the monitor around to face us as she confirmed the oncologist's report with the images on the screen.

Knowing I had done everything possible, I trusted God with the outcome and His will for my life.

"You have a large mass on your left lung, and it seems to be an aggressive type of cancer. There's a slight chance it's inflammation, but it's highly unlikely. We need to remove a portion of your left lung and several lymph nodes as soon as possible."

No! I silently screamed. *I can't have cancer again! That's not possible!* My mind refused to accept the words spilling out of her mouth. I went into total denial.

"Can we do a biopsy to be sure?" I asked.

"That is not an option. The risk of your lung collapsing is too great."

Filled with despair, I fought back tears as I headed to the front desk to schedule the surgery. The Holy Spirit heavily pressed me to consider the possibility of inflammation. *How could these doctors be so confident it wasn't inflammation without further testing? Why not look at the possibility?*

The receptionist booked the procedure for the end of the month. Choking back tears, I agreed on the date. Once we were outside, I fell into my friend's arms and sobbed.

"I can't believe this is happening again." But then I remembered the nudge from the Holy Spirit. "I have three weeks until my surgery date. I need a second opinion. I'm not comfortable with this."

When we got in the car, I called my primary care physician. He squeezed me in for an appointment late that afternoon. Saddened to hear my news, he agreed to help rule out inflammation and prescribed a robust ten-day antibiotic. My next call was to my pulmonary specialist. After reviewing the films, he concurred that the area *could* be inflammation.

"I'm not saying this isn't cancer, but cancer is usually denser than the image your films reveal. Finish the antibiotic and we will rescan in a week."

I can't explain it any other way except to say that the Holy Spirit, with great strength, pressed me to refuse the diagnosis of cancer. I questioned why God would bring me through so much, only to let it happen to me all over again in less than a year. And why wouldn't the surgeon take every step possible to rule out inflammation before choosing a hundred-thousand-dollar surgery?

Worse, there was a good chance I might not live through this kind of surgery. I had smoked most of my life. By the time I stopped, I had COPD. My pulmonary doctor had put me on an inhaler and continued to monitor nodules on both my lungs for the past several years. No doubt this would be a dangerous procedure for me.

I finished the antibiotic, and my lungs were rescanned. Knowing I had done everything possible to ensure accurate results, I trusted God with the outcome and His will for my life.

My phone rang, and the familiar voice of my primary care physician on the other end of the line reported, "Your scans came back. The new images reveal that the area of concern has shrunken by half. Cancel your surgery. You definitely do not have cancer. You can pick up your films in the morning and bring them to your surgeon."

I questioned why God would bring me through so much, only to let it happen to me all over again in less than a year.

"Thank you! Thank you! Thank you! I can't tell you how grateful I am to you for taking the time to see me on such short notice, rush tests, and provide me with results so quickly."

When I showed the films to the surgeon, she compared them to her own, and the difference was staggering. It appeared the mass had broken up into the shape of a V.

"This is good news for you. I'm sorry, but sometimes we make mistakes. I will alert the tumor board and cancel the surgery."

This experience confirmed for me the importance of listening to the Holy Spirit's prompting and the occasional need for a second opinion.

Oh, but how good is God? He fashioned a course to divinely use vanity as a method to discover cancer in my kidney. He led me to a doctor who was careful enough to do that preliminary testing before surgery where others might not, and to doctors who took the time to listen and compassionately care for me. I give glory and praise to God for keeping me wrapped in His undeniable protection.

The Mysteriously Postponed Trip

Doug Baker, as told to Mindy Baker

Many are the plans in a person's heart,
but it is the LORD's purpose that prevails.

—PROVERBS 19:21 (NIV)

When the Covid-19 pandemic hit in 2020, the scope of my job immediately changed. Instead of traveling on exciting overseas adventures, our mission organization was forced to begin doing all of our work virtually. Before Covid, my coworker and I traveled multiple times a year to various countries in order to coach and to train Christian leaders in person and to observe and experience their ministries firsthand in some of the least-reached regions of the world. The pandemic forced us to do our training sessions virtually. The virtual training was better than nothing, but it wasn't the same. I missed the fellowship of the one-on-one personal interactions and training leaders face-to-face.

To my surprise, rather than being detrimental to our ministry, the virtual option increased our reach exponentially. Now we have ministry partners in many more countries and languages and have even expanded our ministry to an entirely different continent. The Covid virtual sessions led our organization to develop an online learning management system for our international leaders to use. When it is finished, it will enable individuals anywhere in the world to complete our training online. This continues to take much time to write, translate, and produce. We still travel internationally, but not as much.

That is why I was thrilled when an opportunity materialized to go and meet with one of our ministry leaders in Asia. I realized how much I wanted to do an overseas trip, especially to a location that I had never traveled to before. I was elated when my board of directors approved the proposed trip.

However, the board had one condition: they wanted me to find someone to travel with me. The coworker I normally travel with did not feel that he should go, as he was deeply involved in the writing process of the learning management system and wanted to continue that work. I prayed fervently about who to ask. As names came to mind, I made many phone calls. I invited at least a dozen men, but no one could go. Still, I persisted. In faith, I booked my flight without a travel partner, continuing to pray that one would materialize. Finally, after much conversation, I convinced my coworker to take a break from his writing, and he agreed to go with me.

Yet as we prepared to go, none of the details were falling into place easily. The final straw was when I realized that we needed to purchase travel visas before the trip and had not done so. I had planned to obtain them upon arrival, but after consulting with some experts who had traveled many times to our destination, I learned we needed them before our departure. There was simply not enough time for the visas to reach us by mail.

In the middle of a spring break trip with my wife, I informed her that we were going to have to change our plans and drive to Washington, DC, to obtain the needed visa. She looked at me with a bewildered expression on her face and said, "Are you sure you are supposed to go on this trip?"

The question made me stop and reconsider everything. Was God trying to tell me something by placing these roadblocks in my way? In the midst of this critical moment, my coworker called. We talked extensively and agreed to pray about it separately for thirty minutes. He had set up a group phone call with our ministry partner in Asia to discuss the problem with him. At the end of the call, I remember my coworker's conclusion: "I don't think the timing is right. Let's hold off on it and plan to go in the fall." I felt sick to my stomach. I had been so sure that I was supposed to go. I wanted to serve God. *Why is every door shutting?*

A few weeks later, God's reason for the roadblock became apparent. My father-in-law had been battling a brain disease for several years, but to our knowledge, he was not in any immediate distress. We live about eight hours away from them in a different state. My mother-in-law, his faithful caretaker, normally would visit my father-in-law daily in the nursing home. However, she had recently fallen while visiting him and was suffering a brain bleed that necessitated a stay in a nearby hospital. We were not prepared for the ripple effect that this would cause.

One Friday night as we were watching TV, my wife received a phone call. It was her father's nurse telling her that her father could no longer swallow any water. He had reached the final stage of his disease, and would most likely pass away in the next ten days. After hanging up the phone, my wife fell into my arms, heartbroken. She immediately began making plans to travel and see him.

One week later, my wife's father passed away. If I had been overseas as I had planned, I would not have been able to comfort her during her time of deep loss. Looking at the calendar, I not only would have missed the critical phone call in which she received the shocking news, but I also would not have been able to attend the funeral. She later expressed to me how much it meant to her that I was there for her during this difficult time.

She looked at me with a bewildered expression on her face and said, "Are you sure you are supposed to go on this trip?"

I was humbled by God's provision for my wife and was reminded that His ways are higher than my ways. When the plans I make don't work out the way I think they should, I need to be patient and trust that there is a reason for it. In this case, God had my wife wrapped in His protection. He knew that she would need me by her side. I am thankful for God's perfect timing.

God's Call to Come Home

June Foster

*And my God will meet all your needs according
to the riches of his glory in Christ Jesus.*

—Philippians 4:19 (NIV)

My husband, Joe, and I have a passion for travel, often embracing the full-time RV lifestyle. Over the years, we've rented out our home and set off on adventures that surpassed our wildest dreams. But a few years ago, the unthinkable happened. If it weren't for God's mighty hand and His call to come home, I'm not sure how we would've made it.

I loved the RV lifestyle. With just one frying pan, two pots, and a single baking dish, we prepared countless delicious meals. My husband frequently took to the outdoors, grilling on the picnic table, adding a special touch to our culinary adventures. Another perk? I could clean our entire RV in just forty-five minutes, a stark contrast to the three to four hours I worked to tidy up our house. No housekeeper would complain about that.

And we visited so many incredible places. Joe often said that traveling in the RV felt like being on a permanent vacation, and I wholeheartedly agreed.

During nearly twenty years of exploration, we've ventured to Philadelphia, where we stood before the Liberty Bell, wandered through Independence Hall, and visited Betsy Ross's house, along with one of the nation's oldest churches. We journeyed down the coast to the Wright Brothers National Memorial in Kitty Hawk, North Carolina. One of our most memorable trips followed the Lewis and Clark Trail, retracing the explorers' steps as closely as possible to their original route. We began in Missouri and traveled the historic pathway to the end at the mouth of the Columbia River near present-day Astoria, Oregon, ensuring we didn't miss any museums or landmarks along the way.

Through the years we always had a home base. We owned a house in Lacey, Washington, where we'd moved after I retired from teaching. Since the RV bug had bitten us, we rented out our home and hit the road. About fifteen years into the RV lifestyle, we decided to change our homebase to Cullman, Alabama, where Joe was born and raised. We were attracted not only by the personal history but by Alabama's economy and warmer weather. We purchased a house but once again rented it out and went traveling in our RV.

For the year 2020, we planned to make Acadia National Park in Maine our first destination. Then, at the end of 2019, an unexpected urge nudged me to return to Cullman. My heart said, *Go home and settle down.*

I told Joe about my impressions, and he didn't take me seriously at first. But then, a few days later, the same impulse pressed upon his thoughts.

We'd heard rumors of Covid-19 but didn't fully grasp the impact the disease would have on our country. We decided we should live in Alabama until any potential danger passed. With a renter still in our old house, we purchased another home and moved into our new dwelling in the summer of 2020. We figured that when the time came to travel again, we would rent out our new house and head out.

Life in our new small-town community brought us joy as we found a welcoming church and met many wonderful people. Nevertheless, the old desire to travel lingered in the back of our minds.

---

*Five months after moving into our new house,
the reason for our return became clear.*

Before Christmas in 2020, Joe began to notice blood in his urine and experienced frequent urination. He made an appointment with a local urologist who ordered a lab test. In January 2021, five months after moving into our new house, the reason for our return became clear. A few days into the new year, Joe received the daunting news that he had bladder cancer. Remaining close to medical care was now essential, and it ruled out any further travel for the time being. Joe began treatment, requiring weekly trips to the doctor's office for six weeks, followed by regular check-ups every four months to monitor his health.

After a year of treatment with Joe's local doctor in Cullman, his original urologist recommended a specialist in bladder cancer who practiced in Birmingham, about forty miles south of us. Joe began weekly trips to Kirklin Clinic.

One evening during this time, we reflected upon the past couple of years. Only God could've orchestrated these events: leading us to Cullman when He did, offering protection from a world pandemic, and providing us a doctor who specializes in bladder cancer at the very time Joe needed the medical help.

The good news is that my husband is now in remission, though he still sees the urologist in Birmingham regularly. We purchased a smaller RV and still travel, but our trips are now mostly near home.

Looking back, had we not settled down, our situation might have turned out differently. If we found ourselves in Maine in Arcadia National Park, Joe might have ignored his symptoms, choosing to continue with our travels. Or perhaps we would have fled to Bar Harbor for help. Beginning treatment so far away from home might not have been the best decision. God watched over us, providing the direction we needed before we even knew about the diagnosis.

I'll always cherish the amazing experiences we had in our RV, but I'm even more grateful for the care and protection our Lord and Savior provided us, His children.

Just in Time

Debbie Simmons

—⁂—

*If I rise on the wings of the dawn, if I settle on the
far side of the sea, even there your hand will guide
me, your right hand will hold me fast.*

—PSALM 139:9–10 (NIV)

Finally, I was on my paddleboard again.

I'd been thrilled when my daughter found out she
was pregnant after years of trying to have a child—but
she was also in the process of adopting a baby at the time, and
she ended up giving birth just four months after the adoption
was finalized. Having two infants was a handful, and I was
more than willing to help. However, I'd been so busy caring
for them that the time had flown by, and it had been a year
since I had a chance to enjoy paddling on the bay and bayous
near my home in the Florida panhandle.

Recently, though, I'd been craving the chance to get out on
the water again, so I scheduled a day and time for a friend
to meet me and paddleboard together. I was determined to
keep that date, but circumstances conspired to slow me down.
First, a discussion with my husband at breakfast took longer
than I expected, then I ended up in rush-hour traffic, such

as it is in our small community. Finally reaching the agreed-upon spot, I unloaded my board and waited for my friend. And waited. And waited. I have to admit I was miffed by then, and when I texted her to find out where she was, I was even more irritated to find out she couldn't make it. Resisting the impulse to send an ugly answer, I prayed, *God, help me to not be angry with my friend. Thank you for the opportunity to go paddleboarding again. I'm glad that I have You as a companion.*

Because I hadn't paddled for a while, I initially planned to stay close to shore. But when I saw other paddleboarders and several kayakers on the calm water, I followed an

---

Now that I was close, I realized what providence it was that I'd seen him.

---

impulse to alter my route and head for the open water of the bayou. I watched as another paddler helped two guys right a small sailboat that had capsized. Thankful he was there to help them, I continued on, scanning the water for boat wakes so I wouldn't be caught off guard by the motion as the sailors had been.

That's when I saw him. I wasn't sure what it was at first, but as I got closer, I realized that it was a swimmer, splashing and bobbing, obviously struggling—right in the middle of the bayou, where the boat traffic usually goes. I glanced around, thinking surely there was someone else who could help him. But there was no one—except me. Overcoming my usual reluctance to talk to strangers, I paddled toward him. When he went under, my chest tightened, and I paddled hard to get there faster.

Lord, give me strength and balance, I prayed.

He came up to the surface and attempted to float on his back. My arms ached from the strain and my heart raced, but I paddled even harder to speed up, finally reaching him. As soon as I was close enough to speak, I asked, "Do you need help?"

He appeared dazed, but managed to say, "Yes, please. I don't think I can make it."

Now that I was close, I realized what providence it was that I'd seen him. From his exhausted, disoriented body language I figured he had only about five minutes of energy left before he couldn't keep his head above water anymore. "Pull yourself up on the board," I told him. "I'll take you wherever you need to go."

When he told me where he'd started from, I was shocked. It was a mile away!

He sat on the board to rest as I paddled him back, and we made light conversation. Our community has an Air Force base and a Department of Defense training facility, as well as special operations training venues. These programs are physically demanding, and as a result, those who participate are in excellent physical health. This young man, Mark, was one of them. He had been at a picnic on the base when his friends dared him to swim a certain distance and back, which would have totaled three miles. Overestimating his stamina, he had gone as far as he could before his strength ran out. I could tell he was embarrassed at needing to be rescued, even more so that he had to accept help from a petite, 65-year-old woman. But I told him that God had put me right there at that time to help him.

When we got near the shore where his friends waited, he slid off and swam over to them. I jokingly told them I couldn't resist picking up such a good-looking man, hoping the humor would save him some embarrassment. Everyone laughed, and we parted ways.

As I reflected on the experience while paddling back to my truck, I realized how perfectly God had arranged everything: the delays on my way to the beach, the friend who never showed but kept me waiting on the shore until just the right moment to leave. Even the impulse to go out into deeper water instead of sticking to the shore had been God at work, leading me to exactly where I needed to be to save Mark's life. I'd started the day just grateful to be going out on the water, and God had led me to a greater joy than I could ever have anticipated.

God's Mysterious Ways: Trusting God's Timing

How often do we need to hear that our thoughts are not God's thoughts, and our ways are not God's ways, before we begin to believe it? We're so used to instant everything, from coffee to speedy delivery of online orders, that we've started to expect the same from communication from God. But He knows what He's doing. He sees the whole picture. When our desires are delayed—or even denied—trusting God's plan can reveal His heart.

- **Pray.** When you pray, ask God to help you trust His timing and to remember that He is a good Father and He has a good plan. One prayer that works well is "Give me patience, Lord."

- **Seek.** Look for ways to serve others as you wait on God's timing for a new job, or a desired relationship, or a new home. There are so many ways we can turn our attention to what's outside of us and needing our attention rather than what's inside, feeding our discontentment.

- **Act.** Each morning as you wake up, give your desires to God, and then go about your day, trusting that He works all things together for our good and His glory.

- **Reflect.** How have you seen God's faithfulness and provision in the past? How can that help you trust that He will continue to be faithful and abundantly provide all that you need?

Sixty Candles

Bobbi L. Graffunder

---

*Even to your old age and gray hairs I am he, I am
he who will sustain you. I have made you and I will
carry you; I will sustain you and I will rescue you.*

—Isaiah 46:4 (NIV)

The summer sun heated the rocks under my fingers. As I
pushed aside the stones to expose the roots of invasive
weeds, I prayed for my mom. Our relationship had been
in a rocky place since my dad died. Neither of us was grieving
well, and it was hard to watch my mom spiral into someone I had
never known before. As I asked God what I could do to help
her, two words lit up like a neon sign. *Affirm her.*

Was this God's answer to my prayer?

As I pondered the meaning of those words, I remembered
that her sixtieth birthday was a few calendar pages away.
A party—a surprise party—would certainly affirm her. On
a whim, I counted off sixty days before her actual sixtieth
birthday and landed on Sunday, September 12. That didn't
leave much time, but it was workable. Leaving the weeds for
another day, I called a couple of my mom's closest friends
and began planning. The party would be easy, but keeping it a
surprise would be hard.

With no time to waste, we booked the church, ordered the cake, and sent out invitations. Sixty individuals were asked to plan a unique way of affirming and honoring my mom. Each person was given a number from one through sixty and asked to weave that number into their presentation. That took care of entertainment and ensured active participation. Everyone was on board with the opportunity to give something back to this woman who had touched so many lives. I was sure it would be a party everyone would remember for years to come.

Everything seemed to be falling into place until everything started falling apart. There were moments of panic when my mom told me someone had invited her to go out of town that weekend. Other times, I received phone calls beginning with, "Your mom just told me . . ." or "We have a problem." These situations required quick action to get her uninvited to another activity or quick thinking to avoid some other catastrophe. There also were struggles with logistics and multiple near misses when someone almost revealed the secret. Inevitably, there were tears, frustrations, and hurt feelings. On more than one occasion, even my mom was upset because she sensed something was going on behind her back.

It didn't take long for my heart to become discouraged. As the date approached, I was convinced I had heard God wrong or at least failed to carry out His plans. I regretted the whole idea, but I had only myself to blame.

Finally, the morning of the party arrived. Instead of being excited, I woke up and thought, *This was a huge mistake. It's too late to cancel, so let's get it over with.* With that, I pushed back the covers and prepared for the disappointment I was sure I would face.

Shortly before leaving for the party, I was alone in my mom's house and noticed a perpetual calendar on the bathroom counter. It had been part of a gift basket I gave her for Christmas. Last summer, the first summer after my dad died, we took a trip to Montana, where she became obsessed with anything and everything huckleberry. While holiday shopping at our local Christian bookstore, this particular calendar jumped out at me because the cover was the exact color of

---

When I saw those words staring back at me on that day of all days, my fears and anxiety completely melted away.

---

huckleberry purple. For that reason alone, I added it to the assortment of huckleberry-themed gifts I gave her.

My heart jumped when I saw the September 12 verse of the day: "Even to your old age and gray hairs I am he, I am he who will sustain you. I have made you and I will carry you; I will sustain you and I will rescue you" (Isaiah 46:4, NIV). I immediately started crying. "I'm sorry, God. I am so sorry I doubted you," I sobbed.

This particular verse held special meaning for my mom and dad. Years earlier, when my mom found her first gray hair, my dad gave her a bracelet engraved with that exact Bible verse. She wore it regularly, even more often after my dad died, and we always paid special attention on the rare occasions that we came across that verse. When I saw those words staring back at me on that day of all days, my fears and anxiety completely melted away. I had heard God after all; beyond a shadow of a doubt, this was His confirmation.

How could it be a mere coincidence? I didn't know that verse would show up on September 12. I didn't know it was even in that calendar to begin with. I only chose that date because it was sixty days before my mom's sixtieth birthday. I only chose that calendar because it was purple. Also, because it was a perpetual calendar, it had been printed long before I purchased it, possibly even before my dad passed away.

The party was a roaring success from start to finish. My mom was powerfully affirmed, but she wasn't alone. Each person had poured great love into the gifts they prepared and shared. Poems were read, songs were sung, stories were told, and tears were cried. I stood at the back of the room and took it all in. Sixty candles illuminated my mom's smile as friends and family surrounded her. Each flame represented our power to encourage and lift one another up when life gets hard.

I was overwhelmed by it all. The party was supposed to be a surprise for my mom, but God had a surprise in store for me. My faith was affirmed, but I also realized what I would have missed if I had given in to discouragement and doubt. All along, God knew the significance the day would bring. Even in the moments when I wanted to give up, He was working behind the scenes. Some might call it a big coincidence, but I see the fingerprints of God weaving details together into a beautiful tapestry of His faithfulness. Surprise!

Two Norms and the Planters of Peace

Ingrid Skarstad

As a father has compassion on his children, so the LORD has compassion on those who fear him; for he knows how we are formed, he remembers that we are dust. The life of mortals is like grass, they flourish like a flower of the field.

—PSALM 103:13–15 (NIV)

My tiny Prius was packed to the gills—or at least to the backs of the front seats. Sunrise had broken the Oklahoma horizon hours before, which meant I was already behind schedule on my trek to Minnesota.

I looked around to see what else I could use to fill the remaining space in the front seat. A large yellow pot by the door caught my attention. The tropical palm within it had not survived the months I had been away while caring for my father in his last days.

An idea flashed through my imagination. I had noticed mint-like plants coming up among the weeds on the shore of the lake outside Dad's house that spring. They tasted like mint too. *Maybe I could transplant it?* I needed to clean the shoreline anyway, since Dad was gone.

I pulled on the trunk of the leafless palm, and it released the dirt easily. *Oh good! Dirt to go!* I plopped the bright planter ready with soil into the front seat. *Happy color.* I plucked up two more planters that hovered in a cubby space, waiting to be filled. *I'll fill them all with mint!*

Happiness was a welcome change. In the wake of my dad's passing, I craved joy. The yellow pot, suddenly a vessel of hope, gave me something to smile about: Dad's accidental "lake mint" thriving (hopefully) in my happy planter.

With my car sufficiently full, I sat down behind the wheel and asked, "Lord, where should I stay along the way?" I knew I couldn't make the fourteen-hour drive in one go, not if I was starting late in the day. I also knew from previous trips that I couldn't count on grabbing a hotel along the way.

I got quiet. Listened. Phone ready. Priceline was on my screen ready to make a hotel reservation.

"Aurora" floated to my mind. *Aurora?* It wasn't familiar to me.

I googled and found four Auroras near my possible routes. Only one location brought up a hotel—five miles away in Brookings, South Dakota. I especially love to support small-town economies. *I'll at least go to Aurora for lunch. Maybe they have a little deli.* Surely God had something special in the tiny town.

The "Aurora adventure" distracted me from my unrest about the other challenges I faced.

After my dad passed, I made regular trips to Minnesota from Oklahoma to handle affairs and help my disabled brother. I carried my work with me, and when I was at Dad's place on the lake, I preferred to work on my laptop at his picnic table outside. Nature was my insulation from chaos.

My late father's home itself was organized, and his estate was not hard to manage. He had prepared well. He also invited my son to live with him and then stay in the house after he passed. That's where chaos entered, and her name was Synneva—the adopted rescue mutt my son eagerly accepted now that Grandpa wasn't there to say no. The bright-eyed dog had already destroyed the carpets and anything with an exposed electrical cord.

Norm? That's my dad's name!
It was enough of a sign for me!

Peace was easiest to enjoy on the road between homes. My daughter's growing family had moved in with me while trying to find a home. I was glad to have someone to watch the house while I traveled, but I wasn't prepared for the mayhem of mess again! It multiplied with married children, grandchildren, and pets! I savored slow travel and staying overnight when I could.

I checked in at Brookings and settled in for the next day's adventure.

That morning, I googled "deli Aurora SD." Nothing. OK . . . "restaurants"? None! Had I misunderstood God on this "Aurora" thing?

I zoomed in on Google maps to check out the little town. What *was* there?

A large plot of land was colored green on the border of the town. I zoomed in more and read, "Norm's Greenhouse and Nursery."

Norm? That's my dad's name! It was enough of a sign for me! My dad spent his life in agriculture—Peace Corps, agriculture education, crop insurance. Could he be orchestrating this from heaven? I didn't really believe that, but the thought made me smile.

I set my GPS on the nursery and drove through four miles of farmland. Before I reached Aurora, a left turn came up on the screen. I followed a dirt road that disappeared into the trees and transformed into a magical lane.

I had expected a traditional nursery, just greenhouses and such, but I could see none as I drove down the secluded road and found a place to park. Behind the lush greenery, potted plants exploded around the property, placed along paths that led to greenhouses that were hidden to the outside world. I felt as if I had found a secret garden! I embarked upon the nearest winding path though a sea of blossoms.

A middle-aged man in khakis found me meandering in my citified clothing and asked if he could help me find something specific.

"I don't know what I'm looking for."

He grinned. "Maybe I can help you find something special?"

I told him about my father's place and the small deck that had become my workspace and place of escape—from everything other than mosquitos. "Maybe I could find something that repels them?"

He led me through seemingly endless options, and I chose flowering grasses that should flourish in the zone farther north.

"How did you find out about us?"

I told the tale of "Aurora" and about how "Norm's Greenhouse and Nursery" had popped up when I searched for a hotel or deli. "Norm is my dad's name, so I thought it might be nice to find something for his place, since I will be up there for a while." I paused, then asked, "Are you Norm?"

"No, that's my dad. He passed away in January."

"My dad passed away in December!"

Our fathers shared a similar background, and we laughed in awe about the coincidences we discovered as we shared stories. He knew what it was like to grow up with a dad in agriculture and understood what it means to find peace in nature. Had the two heavenly Norms conspired to bring me here? Somehow, I didn't feel so alone now. It was the first conversation since my dad's death that didn't feel weighted with grief or responsibility. Instead I felt light, as if I was making a space for myself in my dad's world.

Had the two heavenly Norms conspired to bring me here? Somehow, I didn't feel so alone now.

I walked back to my car with the tall, mosquito-repelling grasses swaying in my arms. *Should I plant them in Dad's landscaped beds? Maybe I could replace some plantings along the pathway to the deck?*

As I reached my car and remembered how the interior was packed as snug as a jigsaw puzzle, I wondered if I could even fit the grasses inside! Maybe they could peek up around the big yellow pot if I sat them on the floor?

Nestled below the yellow pot were the two empty blue planters I'd put in the car when I had the idea about the mint. I had forgotten about them! The grasses fit perfectly inside.

"Thank you, Dad," I whispered as I left the peaceful oasis behind, bringing a little of it with me.

She Has a Name

Kristen Paris

———————⬥———————

"I have summoned you by name; you are mine."
—Isaiah 43:1 (NIV)

Perhaps I shouldn't have browsed through that catalog. My propensity to buy things I didn't need had been a way of coping with stress, frustration, and even fear. I'd gotten better over time. It had been quite a while since I'd made an unnecessary purchase, and I wanted to keep that streak going to prove to myself that I wasn't materialistic or frivolous. Besides, we really couldn't afford extras.

But browse I did, and something caught my eye. At least it wasn't for myself this time, or even for our children, who really didn't need anything new.

It was springtime, and a pink tulip design on a two-page spread of merchandise practically sang out the joy of the season of life renewed. The personalized stationery set called out to my inner shopper. A close friend of mine loved pink tulips. This pattern was particularly appealing because it was bordered by a soft spring green, a favorite color of hers. It couldn't have been more well suited to my friend if she had designed it herself.

I hesitated. It wasn't her birthday; that had recently passed. It wouldn't be appropriate for Christmas. But it was perfect for her, and I smiled as I thought of her eyes lighting up in delight. I knew I had to buy it.

My frugal streak withered. I chose a feminine font to personalize it with her name, Debbie, and ordered. These were the days before next-day delivery, so I had to wait several weeks. Patience isn't my strong suit, and I think I was more anxious over this simple gift than I'd ever been for anything I'd ordered for myself. This purchase just felt right, and I hoped it was as pretty in person as it was in the catalog.

The box finally came, and I ripped it open excitedly. The stationary was gorgeous, exceeding my expectations, and I couldn't wait to give it. I knew I should save it for Christmas. But it was May. Christmas was a long time away.

I debated. Now that I had it in my hand, my impulse purchase seemed a bit silly. I knew she'd love it, but there wasn't an occasion to celebrate, or a natural opportunity to give it to her. Why had I caved to an impulse when I'd been so good lately about not spending money? Guiltily, I took it to the "gift closet" where I hid Christmas gifts from our kids, but then I couldn't bring myself to hide it away there. After all, the purchase had been made, and I couldn't send it back, because it was personalized. Mostly, though, I just ached to give it to her. Now.

I hadn't heard from my friend for a little while, which was unusual. We used to get together often for coffee, tea, or walks through the pine forest near my home. But lately, she had been a bit more distant. Uncertain whether I should bother her, I stood indecisively for several minutes. Finally, I wrapped the set in a pretty gift bag with pink tissue paper, headed to her house, and left it on the doorstep. I was pretty sure she'd know who it was from.

I was correct.

A few days later, we walked together again, meandering down our favorite trail as we hadn't done for a while. The pensive mood she'd been in lately seemed lifted a bit, and she opened up about the downward spiral her thoughts had been taking recently. With tears in her eyes, she told me what my small gift had meant to her.

The day I brought it over, she had hit her lowest point. The feeling had been looming for some time, growing in the deep recesses of her heart where no human eye sees. Like many a homeschool mom at the end of her teaching tenure, she'd been feeling useless and unnecessary. Her kids were nearly grown, and technically didn't need her to get through the motions of daily life anymore. As a stellar homemaker, her life revolved around family. Those of us who serve our loved ones day in and day out as our primary occupation are particularly affected by normal life changes like children growing up and depending on us less. Without performance reviews, raises, or office meetings where we can be seen, it's easy to feel insignificant, even worthless. This can lead to questioning of one's value and purpose in living.

With tears in her eyes, she told me
what my small gift had meant to her.

"My husband would be fine without me. My kids are self-sufficient. They don't need me. They'd be fine too," she told me.

"I had a plan," she whispered hesitantly, tears welling in her eyes. That got my attention, and she was no longer the only one with tears in her eyes. I wondered how I had missed seeing her grief and desperation. She didn't expand on her "plan," and I didn't ask, as it felt too personal. I understood. Life had no longer seemed worth continuing. I'd been in that dark place too at times. I knew that empty feeling all too well.

Her tone grew more hopeful. "When I saw your gift, it reminded me—I have a name."

She repeated the statement as tears spilled over for both of us.

"I have a name."

In a stronger tone, with a tentative but heartfelt smile, she continued, "I am known. I am significant. I mean something to someone. I'm not nobody. I have a name."

To this day, I don't know exactly how deep her depression went in that season. These things are hard to fully understand when we're not the one going through them, no matter how deeply we love those who are. But God knows. He saw her. He heard her heart's cry. And He answered through a simple set of stationery, emblazoned with her name.

I wondered what might have happened had I not fallen prey to my shopping habit. What if I had been strong, resisting the urge to purchase something totally unnecessary by any practical standard? I've since learned to throw catalogs away without looking at them, though online shopping makes overspending a constant temptation. But I'm grateful for that one slip up, when God used my weakness for good.

He saw her need, and knew what would speak to her when that need grew deepest. He'd heard my prayers that I be a tool in His hand and knew exactly how to best use me. He even knew the precise timing that would bring together each detail perfectly, from the day the catalog arrived in the mail to the moment she found the gift on her doorstep.

Years have passed, and our friendship has deepened as we have walked through life together. We've celebrated, mourned, laughed, and yelled in frustration, trusting and caring for each other's hearts. She has helped me far more than I ever could help her, particularly when I've struggled through dark days of my own. I can't count the number of times she has "coincidentally" called at just the right instant to keep me from doing something foolish, or when I needed a listening ear. It may be our friendship, but it's also God's tool for shaping us, comforting us, encouraging us, and sometimes confronting us.

I couldn't have known the unspoken need of my friend's heart, but God did. To me, it was an impulse purchase. From God, it was both a lifeline and a love note.

I ordered a mere gift, but God had ordered my steps.

She has a name: a name God knows. So do you.

Heart-Shaped Rocks

Lynne Hartke

*Keep your heart with all vigilance, for from it
flow the springs of life.*

—Proverbs 4:23 (esv)

My friend Jeff often sends me photos of heart-shaped objects he sees out in nature.

"I saw another heart-shaped leaf on my walk this morning," he would write. The accompanying photo backed up his words. "I felt it was a smile from my dad."

Jeff and I had connected a decade earlier at a cancer event when the disease had touched both our families. After his dad and both my parents died from cancer, we had maintained our friendship. Unlike Jeff, when I saw heart-shaped things out in nature, I never tied heavenly messages to their existence nor saw them as a way to process grief.

But then I started seeing my own heart-shaped rocks. Did God have a message for me?

Mollie, our rust-colored terrier mix, had been part of the family for thirteen years. A pound rescue, she had hiked with my husband, Kevin, and me all over Arizona. She instinctively gave rattlesnakes a wide berth and would lift her paw and wait for me to extract any random cactus thorns from her paw.

At her last vet appointment—seven months before—she had wowed everyone with my stories of seven-mile hikes and adventures in the wilderness. Her long coat was only starting to show signs of white hair.

When I brought her back to the vet with troubling symptoms, I expected to hear that she was finally slowing down. The last thing I expected the vet to tell me was that Mollie did not have years or even months to live. She only had hours.

I could not believe my adventure buddy was gone.

We have always been a dog family, but after the loss of Mollie, I was not ready to consider another pet. I needed time.

And I had stipulations.

"We will not get a big dog," I declared. "We will get another thirty-pound dog like Mollie."

I also had a timeframe.

"We will wait at least six months until our travel plans are finished and our schedules slow down."

On these two things I was adamant.

"Don't close your heart to a dog that may show up in our lives unexpectedly," Kevin advised as I packed to go to our cabin six weeks after Mollie died. He reminded me of the times two of our grown children had acquired dogs that had simply wandered into their yards. Our kids had hung "Found Dog" flyers around the neighborhood, posted on lost-dog social media sites, and made sure the dogs did not have microchips. When all their efforts failed, Socks and Fennie had become part of their families.

"I'm not ready for another dog," I told him firmly.

At the cabin, I unloaded the suitcase, a cooler, and a box of research books for several writing projects. I picked up the dog bowls on the kitchen floor and rolled up Mollie's blanket from under our bed.

"The cabin is too quiet without Mollie," I told Kevin when I texted him to let him know I had arrived safely.

The next morning, my brain refused to focus on the words on my computer. I slept badly. In the silent cabin, every creak and noise seemed to be amplified. I woke three times in the night, listening in vain for Mollie's dog tags.

In the gravel, exactly where the squirrel had sat, was a heart-shaped black stone embedded in the road.

Needing to escape the four walls, I decided to stretch my legs with a walk to a nearby water tower in the ponderosa pine forest. Stellar jays squawked above me in the branches of the trees while a red squirrel searched for acorns for the upcoming winter.

"If Mollie were here, she would lead you on a merry chase," I said as the squirrel headed for its home in a dead tree. In the gravel, exactly where the squirrel had sat, was a heart-shaped black stone embedded in the road. I had never noticed it before.

That's interesting. But I didn't give the rock a second thought.

In the afternoon, I headed to Mayflower Springs, a three-mile hike. The last time I had been here, Mollie had enjoyed a drink from the natural water source, while I noted a new bird for my birding life list—a red-faced warbler.

There were no birds in sight today, but five sulphur butter-flies flitted around the mountain dandelions, wild roses, and hooker's onion. On a large, flat rock by the spring, someone had left a heart-shaped rock the size of my palm.

A second rock!

God, are you trying to tell me something? I wondered.

Back at the cabin, I scrolled through memories of Mollie on my phone. Mollie in the middle of our canoe on a nearby lake. Mollie in the morning mist at the cliff edge. Mollie in a field of wildflowers with her laughing eyes and tongue out. The cabin had been her happy place.

The next day, I decided to hike part of the Arizona Trail behind the cabin. Instinctively, I reached for the blue leash that still hung by the front door, only to pull back my hand as if slapped.

Why was grief so hard?

Determined to enjoy the morning, I headed to a section of the trail known for an abundance of wildflowers. A tiny cliff chipmunk darted ahead of me on the path before diving into a cluster of Indian paintbrush. As I bent to take a picture of the red flowering spikes, I saw another heart-shaped rock.

"OK, God, one rock I could ignore. Two rocks, I could wonder. But three? You have my attention! Is there a message I need to hear?" I spoke the words aloud, disturbing two ravens from the nearby trees. Their raucous calls interrupted the silence as they took to the air currents above me.

I thought of Kevin's advice to not shut my heart to another dog. Was that the message of the heart-shaped rocks? *Impossible*, I thought, but I remembered the words from another friend who often rescued animals.

"Don't be afraid to love again," she had written when she heard about Mollie. "The best way to honor the memory of a beloved fur baby is to pass on the love to another who needs a family and a forever home."

Don't be afraid to love again. Could I do it?

That night, scrolling on my phone, I saw a post about an eight-month-old sheepadoodle, an English sheep dog and standard poodle mix. Staring into the puppy's eyes, something inside me stirred. The family needed to move and rehome the dog immediately. The puppy weighed fifty-one pounds. I sent Kevin the information. He called me back immediately.

My heart was conflicted. A possible new beginning warred with the grief of a difficult ending I was still processing. How could both exist in the same heart?

"Why are you sending me a dog photo?" he asked.

"I want to go look at that puppy," I told him.

"What about your rules about not getting a big dog and waiting six months?" he countered.

"I just want to check her out," I said, "I'm not committing to anything. I have an appointment when I get back tomorrow."

The next day, we met Sadie, a nervous, shaggy pup with gentle manners and curious eyes. Upon seeing her, I expected to be filled with overwhelming joy. And if not joy, at least a sense of peace, a knowing that she was the one for us. That was not the case.

My heart was conflicted. A possible new beginning warred with the grief of a difficult ending I was still processing. How could both exist in the same heart?

Sadie nudged my hand, her tail down, also unsure.

I thought of the three heart-shaped rocks I had found, messages I now knew were from my heavenly Father—an invitation to love again.

"We will take her," I said.

God's Mysterious Ways: A Message from the Heart

Have you ever had the experience of seeing a message from God all over the place once He has first brought it to your attention? It's like when you buy a new car and suddenly you see that same car on the road way more often than you did before. Like the heart-shaped rocks from the story you just read, there are images, Bible verses, certain words God emphasizes to speak to our hearts.

- **Pray.** Each day you can take the opportunity to pray and ask God what it is that He wants to build into you. We're all works in progress, needing to grow in different areas. Let God know your heart is open to His pruning and molding so that you can be more like Jesus.

- **Seek.** Look for patterns. What do you keep seeing, hearing, or reading that might just be God trying to speak into your heart?

- **Act.** Once you notice patterns, take some time to listen to God about how He wants to refine you in that area. Like in our story of the heart-shaped rocks, Lynne needed to be open to adopting another dog even in the midst of her grief over losing her previous beloved dog. What change do you need to make in light of what God is telling you?

- **Reflect.** How can you pay better attention to what's going on around you throughout your day? Pause now and then and take a moment to consciously notice what's around you. Keeping a journal of the things that stand out in your mind can help you see and remember patterns.

Tuning Our Hearts to God's Frequency

Laura Bailey

*We must pay the most careful attention, therefore,
to what we have heard, so that we do not drift away.*

—HEBREWS 2:1 (NIV)

M y phone lit up with a text from one of my closest friends: "Do you want to grab coffee?"

Normally, I would have leapt at the opportunity to pump caffeine in my veins and chat till my jaws hurt, but I didn't feel like it today. And truthfully, I hadn't felt like being around people, even those I loved, for the past few weeks.

I was in a season of intense doubt. I'd decided to say yes to a ministry opportunity that I felt confident God wanted me to pursue, yet things were not going well. I was consumed with feelings of defeat, questioning whether I should throw in the ministry towel completely and pursue an "easier" calling.

My phone dinged again and again. Unable to ignore the constant din, I snatched up my mobile, preparing to decline the invite. But the words on the screen arrested my attention.

"Look, I'm not sure what's happening, but I know you're avoiding me. We need to talk. Let me help you get out of this funk. I am not taking no for an answer."

I shouldn't have been surprised by her message. She was pretty intuitive, but I thought I'd been hiding my foul mood. Apparently I wasn't.

My foot barely had brushed the threshold of our favorite java hangout before my friend clasped me in a big bear hug. "I can't breathe," I playfully chided. But I longed for the embrace to linger; I felt comfort and peace in her arms. We made our way through our first cups of coffee, caught up on our children, traded notes on beauty regimens, and swapped battle stories of mom fails over the past month.

As my friend placed the second cup into my hands, she said, "OK, enough small talk; what's going on with you?"

I shared my recent heartache over a ministry venture that hadn't turned out as I hoped it would. Allowing the tears to flow down my cheeks, I confessed that my faith was wavering. I shared that the deep conviction I once held that we could impact the world was almost nonexistent, and I'd lost hope in ministry in seemingly insignificant, ordinary ways.

She listened as she sipped her coffee, not interrupting me, even as I continued to ramble on. When I finally took a breath, she waited a beat and gently said, "I am sorry you are going through this. Before we go on, let's pray."

In that moment, I was a bit annoyed. I'd just shared some of my deepest, darkest thoughts, and she thought saying sorry and offering to pray would solve my problems. Still, I smiled through the rest of the conversation, listened to her quote Scripture, and prayed with her a few times. Feeling further frustrated at my situation and what I perceived as my friend's inadequacy to help me feel better, I snatched up my purse and said a quick goodbye.

"Wait! Before you go, have you ever heard the song 'Lord, I Need You' by Matt Maher? I think the words would bring you comfort. Look it up."

I controlled the urge to roll my eyes; instead, we shared a brisk hug and I bolted to my car. That was the confirmation I needed to step away from this ministry role. *No one gets it, no one understands what I am going through, and I am done.*

As I recognized the song streaming through the sound system, I froze, my body covered in goosebumps.

But as I started the car, music blared through the speakers. I reached over to turn the radio off, but then I paused.

How is that possible? I distinctly remember turning the volume down on the radio. I'd been talking to my husband as I pulled into the coffee shop; there's no way I would have heard him at this decibel.

And how was it tuned to the local Christian radio station? In my funk, I'd been avoiding anything remotely related to my faith. The fact that the radio was playing praise and worship music baffled me.

As I recognized the song streaming through the sound system, I froze, my body covered in goosebumps. It was the song my friend had suggested I listen to.

The words filled me with emotion. Maher sang of finding rest, of being guided by the Lord, of being supported when you cannot stand. "Lord, I need You, oh, I need You," the chorus ran. "Every hour, I need You."

The Lord hadn't forgotten me. He cared intimately about every detail of my life. It would have been easy to dismiss this as coincidence, but I knew the Lord was speaking to me. He was trying to get my attention.

He had started with my friend. She was so in tune with the Holy Spirit's prompting that she knew instinctively to reach out to me, to encourage me with prayer, and then share the exact song that would be playing in my car that morning.

There were so many little things that day that the Lord placed in my path to remind me of His goodness in all seasons. While the disappointment over my current circumstances was real, so was God's love and faithfulness. We live in a world marked by sin and suffering, and often, when the Lord asks us to walk in obedience and step out in faith, we will face trials and hardship. But that doesn't mean He's forgotten us or is displeased with us.

What started with a text from a concerned sister in Christ led to a candid conversation over coffee, and ended with a song of encouragement that was just what I needed to lift my spiritual fog. All I needed to do was to adjust my heart to hearing God!

Dragonfly Rescue

Glenda Ferguson

---

*But the fruit of the Spirit is love, joy, peace,
forbearance, kindness, goodness, faithfulness,
gentleness and self-control.*

—GALATIANS 5:22–23 (NIV)

It was one of my last summer vacation days, and I thought a shopping trip to a nearby air-conditioned mall would be a fun way to spend the day while also escaping the high Indiana humidity. I had planned on selecting colorful clothes for my twenty-ninth year of teaching fourth grade, but I was in a bleak mood that had persisted all summer, and left my favorite store empty handed.

Admitting defeat, I drove to a KFC restaurant. At the counter, I placed my order for a large iced tea and a sandwich. Only two other customers occupied the spacious dining area, and I sank into the booth farthest from them. While I waited for my food, I sipped on my tea and stared out the window.

Mom was in a long-term care facility in Missouri. Yes, I was grateful that she had survived a series of strokes and was receiving excellent care and speech therapy. Nothing could wipe away Mom's smile, so, of course, she was making new friends. As for me, I was suffering from a bad case of long-distance daughter guilt. I wanted to be there more often and help her regain her lost abilities. Prayers and my faith got me through each of those early days while Mom regained her health, but I really missed our vacation time.

This summer we didn't spend July together in Missouri as was our tradition. When the days were especially humid, we always sought out the coolest spot. We especially enjoyed driving to Deer Creek, a familiar rural area where Mom had grown up. We wore our old tennis shoes for wading into the cool, flowing water. Mom's focus was on the rocks, and each one she picked up was more interesting than the last. The breeze would pick up, and we would almost shiver.

During each visit, we watched the dragonflies flit through the sunshine and shade. They swooped, hovered over the creek water, and even flew backwards. Sometimes, for fun, we imitated their movements. Mom would move her arms in fancy arcs and circles. I splashed through the creek hoping to catch one with my bare hands. As we watched the dragonflies, I told her about the fascinating facts I had learned about them. These fearless stunt pilots are able to fly in any direction because their four wings move independently. And though they'd been around for nearly 200 million years, they had not changed much. Mom just admired the rainbows on their wings.

I could use some rainbows in my life just then. I didn't have much enthusiasm for the new school year like I usually did. My elementary school had changed leadership, familiar colleagues left, and first-year teachers moved in next door. I felt like a dinosaur with old-fashioned methods, clunky equipment, and dated decorations. I was so behind the times in technology, and the newbies let me know it. My ideas were ignored, attempts at friendship went unacknowledged, and my confidence plummeted. My struggles remained my secret. After all, none of my confidantes were around anymore. I pasted on a smile, loved on my students, and suffered silently. I considered retiring from teaching. Lately I felt as if God had drifted far away, and the Holy Spirit had given up guiding me.

One of God's creatures needed help.
I decided to rescue it.

When my sandwich was delivered to my table, I glanced briefly across the room. I thought I saw a dragonfly out the window. That was not unusual; there are ninety-seven species of dragonflies around Indiana. But as I watched more closely, I realized the dragonfly was not outside. It was trapped inside. It flew away from the window, then turned, and hit the glass. Over and over. The nearby customers didn't even notice the dragonfly's struggles.

The KFC had two doors at the entrance, and it would have required precise flying maneuvers to reach this part of the restaurant without harm. Dragonflies possess voracious appetites. Could it have been enticed by the smell of fried chicken? I doubted that it could return to the outdoors without assistance.

One of God's creatures needed help.

That's when I decided to rescue it.

For all that I knew a number of scientific facts about dragonflies, I had no idea what to expect if I tried to get close to it in a confined area. Would it try to bite me? I decided that it was unlikely to cause me any harm. How could I capture it? From my readings, a net was best in the outdoors. All I had were napkins.

Next challenge: transportation. The dragonfly was not in close proximity to the window on my side of the restaurant. This was not like the creek in Missouri where a mature woman scampering around went unnoticed. I could just imagine the video going viral on social media, my fourth-grade students giggling as they shared it.

The trapped insect would need to move closer. I knew who to ask for help. Who I should have been turning to all summer, for all my struggles, instead of repeating negative thoughts over and over in my mind.

I closed my eyes, bowed my head, and whispered my prayer, "God, if you will just have that dragonfly come over closer to me, I will save it. Amen." The answer, at this moment of my life, was of the utmost importance to me. I needed to know that God heard me, and not just about the dragonfly.

When I looked up, I began scanning the windows for the dragonfly. I found it, motionless, on the ledge of the window next to me. *Thank you, God!*

I acted quickly. I gently placed my napkin over the dragon-fly, then wrapped the paper underneath. The dragonfly fluttered against the restricted space as I tried to communicate that it could trust me. I slid over to the end of the booth and got up. With both of my hands cupping the napkin, I bolted for the exit. This was a dragonfly emergency. I used my right shoulder to push open the inner door, then my left to open the outer door.

Next to the entrance was a flat-topped bush about three feet in height. I lowered the napkin to the bush. Very, very carefully, I lifted the napkin with one grand motion, like a magician revealing a surprise. With a rush of wings and a flash of color, the dragonfly took flight, no longer trapped.

I was really proud of myself. This dinosaur of a teacher still had a few tricks up her sleeve when saving an equally ancient creature!

After collecting my things from inside the restaurant and driving home, I thought about what had happened. What were the odds of a dragonfly being trapped at the very KFC I had randomly selected for lunch? Was that dragonfly sent to rescue me? After all, it had reversed my negativity into joy, kindness, faithfulness, and gentleness. It had prompted that simple, whispered prayer that had resulted in an immediate response.

There was no question in my mind—the Holy Spirit had been guiding me all along, guiding me where I needed to be in response to the sadness in my heart. Just like the dragonfly when I released it, my confidence soared. That very small moment in time was something that would impact my life for a long time—and, hopefully, the dragonfly's too.

He Said Yes

Nyla Kay Wilkerson

This is the confidence we have in approaching God: that if we ask anything according to his will, he hears us.

—1 John 5:14 (NIV)

After our children married and moved into their own places, my husband, Dennis, and I began to discuss the possibility of retirement. Of course, finances were a huge part of that discussion, especially because Dennis's retirement savings had been reduced after a couple of sales of his company.

We decided it would be good for our future if I returned to work. That was easier said than done, though. Each day I searched for employment, but nothing seemed to be available. I was underqualified for some jobs and overqualified for others. Then there were jobs that only offered hours that didn't work for me at this time in my life. Dennis and I prayed that the right job would come up, and my prayer partner prayed with me, too. I decided to wait and listen for God's guidance.

One of my favorite places to visit in our town was a Christian bookstore. Being surrounded by Christian music and books while enjoying the company of other Christians was like an oasis in a dry, arid land for me. The atmosphere in the store was peaceful and joyful. I always felt a sense of hope when I read the book titles and cards and examined the beautiful pictures. Workers and customers were normally cheerful and very friendly. The only grumble I ever heard was that there were so few other Christian bookstores in our area.

That got my mind working. Since there was only one Christian bookstore in our area, wouldn't our community need another? For weeks I prayed about opening one, asking the Holy Spirit for His counsel. A sense of peace always followed my prayers, but for some reason it was not the confirmation I needed. I wanted a sign from God confirming this was His will.

Neither party was ready to simply give up;
we decided to seek more definite guidance.

My prayer partner and I diligently prayed for clarity, but God was silent. I did not hear *yes*, *no*, or *wait*. In fact, I couldn't hear Him at all. I realized I needed more information on opening and operating an independent bookstore. Fortunately, our chamber of commerce hosted workshops on how to start a business. They were free, so I attended a few and gleaned valuable information.

It became clear to me that this was not just a whim. My desire was to have a bookstore of my own and provide help to other Christians. The more information I received, the more excited I became to see this idea come to fruition. All I needed was the approval from God.

I found a great space for rent in a strip mall that would be perfect for a bookstore. On one end was a florist and school uniform store while the other housed a brunch restaurant. Was this the yes from God? For some reason, it did not feel like it was the answer I'd been looking for.

Then, I got word from the Christian Booksellers Association that an independent Christian bookstore in a nearby town was closing. I reached out to the store's owners, and they offered a deal on their remaining inventory and fixtures, as well as their counsel.

Before we traveled thirty minutes to see them, my husband and I discussed finances and decided on an amount that we could offer them for their displays and stock. It was not as much as I had hoped, but my husband was leery of risking too much of our savings on this business venture.

We traveled to meet with the owners of the soon-to-close store and see the location in person. The couple was so welcoming and answered our questions honestly. They showed us around their place, noting special items that they were selling or keeping. We were excited and ready to make them an offer. Sadly, it was not enough. They told us the amount they had in mind, and it was far above what we could afford. Was that my answer from God?

Neither party was ready to simply give up; we decided to seek more definite guidance The couple went into another room to pray about a final offer while my husband and I did the same. We asked God to let us know if it was His will that we open a Christian bookstore. I did not want to do anything outside of His plans for my life.

Dennis and I decided we could offer them a little more money because of everything that was included. There was even a neon sign for the window that read Christian Bookstore, and that would save us some money down the road. We prayed and discussed for fifteen minutes before we rejoined the other couple.

The four of us decided that my husband and I would write the highest amount we could pay on a slip of paper, while the sellers wrote the lowest amount they could accept on another slip. When that was done, we traded papers.

When I opened theirs, I stared at it in shock. I looked up and saw that the other couple was just as surprised. The numbers were identical—right down to the penny. This had to be the confirmation from God that I had wanted.

Soon after, with my parents' help, we opened Heaven Help Us Christian Bookstore. As I write this, it has served Christians in our community for ten years. The memories we have made there are priceless. It took some time for me to get the answer I wanted, but when it came, it rang clear and true: He said yes.

The Youth Group That Needed Me

Cecil Taylor

The LORD will guide you always; he will satisfy your needs in a sun-scorched land and will strengthen your frame.

—ISAIAH 58:11 (NIV)

I n my mind, a change was the answer to my misery. Two years out of college, I had not adjusted well to my new city or my first job. Despite regularly attending a medium-sized church, I was lonely and starting to find friends in the wrong places.

My solution was to try to move back to my college town. I interviewed with a prominent computer company, and they made me a job offer. It seemed like the perfect situation: I would make more money and be nearer to family; plus, a lot of my college buddies, including my best friend, were still in town.

I had only to accept the company's offer by the Friday following my interview, and I would be returning to what felt like home.

Being a person of faith, though, I felt like I should pray over the decision. Surely God would see things my way; in fact, I imagined that God had orchestrated the whole move.

So on Tuesday, I prayed for God's guidance. In prayer, I experienced something new and unbelievable: I actually heard God's voice. It said, "That youth group needs you."

To receive a specific, audible response from God was astonishing. But just as surprising was the message. *That youth group needs me? You've got to be kidding, God!*

I had always loved being in youth group growing up. My dad was a small-town pastor, and by age six, I was sneaking into the youth group games and meetings he led—then always getting kicked out. Finally, I became old enough to join youth group, and I immersed myself as much as I could. During my last summer before college, I even led the youth group for three months as our volunteer director took a well-deserved break.

To receive a specific, audible response from God was astonishing. But just as surprising was the message. That youth group needs me? You've got to be kidding, God!

So, it was only natural that when I joined my new church after college, I would eventually become part of the volunteer youth group counselor team. Sadly, it wasn't what I had envisioned. I wasn't given much to do except support the volunteer couple that led the program.

Worse, I was very young-looking, even at age 23, even with the moustache I had grown to look older. A good number of the youth thought I was just another teen.

As far as I was concerned, my impact on this youth group was zero. And God was saying they needed me? I wasn't going to stay in this city for the youth group! That message had to be crossed wires. I decided I would pray about it again on Wednesday.

But the Lord was persistent. On Wednesday, I heard the same voice and same message in prayer. And again on Thursday, this curious message came through yet again. I decided there must be something to the repetition of this miraculous experience.

Without really knowing why the youth group needed me, I reluctantly decided to be obedient to God. I called up the company recruiter and declined the offer. What would I tell family and friends—that God had commanded me in a mysterious voice to stay in town? In the end, I simply told them that I just hadn't given my new city enough of a chance. Then I waited to see what the Lord had in store.

It didn't take long. On Sunday evening, I was sitting in the youth area with my fellow counselor Eugene, another lightly used young volunteer, while we waited for the leading couple to show up for our prep meeting. They arrived late but didn't sit down.

The couple said, "We're burned out. We're leaving now. You two are in charge." They spun and walked out the door.

Eugene and I were both stunned, but my amazement level was higher. God was right: that youth group did need me!

Over the next eight months, Eugene and I led the youth group until the church could secure a full-time youth pastor. The young people bonded with us as they got to know us, and they appreciated how we had stuck with them in a crisis. Those eight months were such fun and so meaningful that I fully committed to youth ministry, to my church, and to my city.

A year later, I became good friends with a new couple in my young adult Sunday school class. Our friendship has continued for decades, and they eventually became my daughter's godparents.

A year after that, I was sitting in that same Sunday school class when a certain young woman walked in. We started out as friends, because after an earlier bad breakup I had set myself a strict policy that I wouldn't date anyone from my church. But one thing led to another, my policy went out the window, and friendship turned into romance. We were married in that church and have been married 40 years. The youth group's handbell choir played at our wedding. Their parents told us how our courtship had modeled Christian dating for their kids.

The couple said, "We're burned out. We're leaving now. You two are in charge." They spun and walked out the door.

As for youth ministry, I continued working as a volunteer there and at a subsequent church for thirty years. Down the line, I was once again called upon to be the volunteer leader of the middle school ministry while the church went through budget cuts; I stayed in that role for four years. Youth work has been one of the best things I've done in my life. I never grew tired of the teens, only leaving when God called me to a new ministry.

I could list dozens of other good things—including career options, connections and friendships, and high-level medical care—that indirectly resulted from my decision to obey God's voice. But the most important thing I learned is that obedience can lead to blessings as God's will is done. When I allowed the Lord to truly be the lord of my life, God blessed that obedience, not solely for my benefit, but for the benefit of so many youth and others over the years.

When God calls, I've learned that I don't need all the reasons. I simply need to listen and follow where God leads me.

God's Mysterious Ways: Hearing His Voice

It's not always easy to hear God's voice, is it? We expect that loud voice out of heaven, like the one that said, "This is my beloved Son. Listen to Him!" But God rarely speaks like that. He uses circumstances, the Bible, and other people to show us what He's trying to tell us. Maybe you've felt that nudge in your spirit. Someone comes to mind when you wake up in the middle of the night, and you think to pray for them right then.

Here are some other things you can do to discern God's voice.

- **Pray.** Ask God to help you hear His voice, and to be open to the different ways He might be trying to communicate with you.

- **Seek.** Look for things that keep cropping up in different ways. You keep seeing a friend's name, or someone will bring them up, or they might even text you out of the blue. What's God telling you in those times?

- **Act.** It can be scary to step out in faith to do what you think God is telling you to do, like the author in the story you just read, who turned down a new job to stay and work with the youth group at his church. But God always equips when He calls. Take that next step of faith.

- **Reflect.** Think about what's been coming up in your life lately. In what ways has God seemed to be getting your attention? Keep asking, seeking, and knocking. He will show you the way.

Listening to God

Linda Marie

After the earthquake came a fire, but the LORD was not in the fire. And after the fire came a gentle whisper.

—1 KINGS 19:12 (NIV)

I n my late twenties I lived in a townhouse on a row that had three other houses. One of my neighbors was a guy, Rick, who was close to my age and very attractive. We became friends. He worked long hours but would stop by sometimes just to talk for a few minutes. During one of those talks, he confided that he used to be hooked on cocaine but had quit and moved to a new area to start his life again. He told me that his addiction began when he played football in high school. One year they won the state championship, and someone brought some cocaine to the afterparty. He tried it that first time, and when they won again the next year, someone brought cocaine again. After that, he couldn't put it down. He didn't give any more details except to say that he had been through terrible things because of drugs. I admired him for being so honest and for working so hard to start a new life.

The two of us got along well, and he even invited me over when his mother, father, and sister came to visit from up north. We played games that weekend and got to know each other. They were such a nice family, and his sister and I had a lot in common.

A few months after meeting Rick, I saw a woman come to his house for the weekend. I was disappointed because I had hoped that he might ask me out. The following weekend he began to act strangely. He would come home in the evening and sit with the blinds in his kitchen open. I worked late, and when I came home from work, I could see him sitting there just staring into the night. One Sunday he raced his Corvette in and out of the parking lot several times during the day and into the night. It was very loud and frightening.

I was worried that he had started to use drugs again and wondered if something bad was going to happen. I had a hard time sleeping. I had been taking a series of classes at church, and I knew the chapel stayed open at night. I went to the church and prayed. At first I wasn't sure what or how to pray. I started with some general prayers I'd learned, like the Lord's Prayer and Hail Mary, and then I began to pray over and over that God would protect Rick and anyone he was involved with. I did what I had heard other people call "praying through." I prayed until I felt a release, a sense that I could go home.

The next morning, there was a knock on my door. It was an older man who worked with Rick, one I had met in passing. He said that Rick had not shown up for work and was not answering his pager. Had I seen him? I knew that this man had befriended Rick; he had taking Rick under his wing, invited him to his house, and taught him about business. He knew about Rick's previous drug problems. He said he was concerned, as I was, that Rick had relapsed. I told him what I had seen, and we agreed to call each other if we learned anything.

An hour later, I was taking my trash to the dumpster behind the townhouses. As I passed Rick's house, I had a very clear and distinct thought that I believe came from God: *Check Rick's back door.*

Walking back to my house, I stopped and knocked on his back sliding-glass door. When there was no answer, I pulled on the handle. The door opened and immediately I felt a hot rush of air that scared me. I closed the door and ran to find

---

As I passed Rick's house, I had a very clear and distinct thought: Check Rick's back door.

---

my neighbor Mary. I told her what happened. We both went back to Rick's house. We pushed open the sliding door and went inside. The door opened to the kitchen, and we discovered that all the burners on the stove were turned on. There was a metal teapot that was so hot it was bright red, and in the middle of the floor was a propane tank surrounded by crumpled-up Coke cans and empty liquor bottles. We immediately turned off the stove. If I had not listened to God and gone in, the building could have blown up.

As Mary and I were trying to understand what was going on, another friend of Rick's, Blake, came to the front door. This person was someone who had grown up with Rick and had transferred to the area at the same time Rick had. Blake said that as soon as he heard Rick was missing, he knew it would be bad. He could see the kitchen, and we told him about turning off the stove. He said he was going to call around and see what happened. He didn't seem surprised or alarmed.

That evening we found out that Rick had had some kind of breakdown. He had gotten into an altercation with someone and was arrested. Later, he was taken to a hospital, then he had flown back to the town where his family lived. Eventually, his things were sent there too, and as far as I know, he never returned.

Through the years, when I think of him, I say a prayer for him and his family. I have often thought of just how dangerous that situation was. I don't think at that moment in time any of us registered the magnitude of what could have happened. I have heard since then that even just opening the door to Rick's kitchen could have caused an explosion if it had generated a spark. I have been so grateful that I was led to pray in particular for protection. I have thanked God over and over for that quiet little voice and the fact that God heard my prayer and protected us all.

Two Nos and a Yes

Betty A. Rodgers-Kulich

God has blocked my way so I cannot move.
He has plunged my path into darkness.

—Job 19:8 (NLT)

A s a Christian college student, life was going as planned. My faith walk was growing, and I had determined to be a disciple of Jesus and dedicate my life to His Kingdom needs. Instead of living on campus, I commuted to school so that I could save money for my upcoming wedding to my high-school sweetheart.

On a crisp, sunny fall Saturday in November, I headed to our rural roadside mailbox to mail my wedding invitations. Excitement bubbled inside of me. It wouldn't be long until I was married. I opened the mailbox only to discover the mail had been delivered earlier than normal. Disappointed with the realization I would need to wait a couple more days to mail the invitations, I grabbed the contents, returning to the kitchen table with mail and invitations in hand.

I perused the mail bundle to see that all but one item were for my parents. But my heart was lifted to find a letter from my fiancé, a US Air Force soldier stationed in Iowa. I tore open the envelope and began to read what my beau had written. Since our wedding was about six weeks away, I was expecting to read how he missed me, his excitement for getting married, and how he was longing to be together as husband and wife.

Instead, I read a normal typical letter of what he had been learning and how the weather was getting colder. He complained that his roommates were annoying, and he couldn't wait to get off base housing. Nothing was out of the ordinary, yet as I read and reread the short letter, I had this gut-level feeling that something was off. I prayed, I reread, I had my parents read the letter, and it seemed only I was troubled. I couldn't explain my feelings, but the more the evening dragged on, the more uneasy I became. I desperately needed to understand why I felt this way.

After dinner, I called Iowa when I knew he should be around to talk. I needed to hear his voice for my peace of mind and to be reassured by his love. The phone rang and rang, until finally one of his roommates answered, informing me that my fiancé was out. They didn't know when to expect him back. I left a message for him to call me when he returned.

Sunday came, and by evening he had not called. I called again only to be told that he still wasn't there. Not understanding where he could be, I let my worry get the best of me. My future suddenly felt dark and ominous. I called his father to see if they had heard from him. His father, with whom I was very close, said they hadn't talked recently, but he would call for me and get him to call me. No call came.

Monday was Veterans Day, and I decided that with school closed, I would go and get to the bottom of why my fiancé wasn't calling me. My worst fear was that he was mangled in some emergency room because he had wrecked his new motorcycle.

Monday came, and right after breakfast, his father drove to our house. As soon as I saw him pull up, I was sure that he was going to tell me that my fiancé was in the hospital. When his father came in, he saw me and immediately hugged me and started crying. When he stopped crying, we sat down. He took my hand, looked me in the eyes, said, "I am so sorry to tell you this . . ." I braced for news of my fiancé's death.

God, did you cause the mailperson to be early that day, so I couldn't mail the wedding invitations?

"My son has been unfaithful to you. He has been living off base with a woman for a couple of months. I only found out late last night by going through some official channel at the air base, telling them there was an emergency at home and my son must call me. When he did, I nailed him on what was going on and he confessed to me. I'm so sorry that I am the one to bring you this news!"

I didn't know if I would kill my fiancé because he was not hurt or because of his unfaithfulness and treachery in stringing me along. He had known I was going to mail the wedding invitations this past weekend. Why would he let me do that if he had no intention of going through with the wedding?

Numbed, I went through several days of fasting and prayer, asking God why He had allowed my fiancé's violation of my love and of the faith that I thought we both shared. Why had my fiancé said no to me? I emptied all my emotions and struggles upon God, feeling like I had been tied up and thrown into a sea of darkness and I was drowning. When I was finally empty, I sat quietly, waiting upon God's comfort for my angry, betrayed heart. In the stillness I began to feel His love, which I allowed so God could mend my heart.

It was then He began to speak to me about my destiny, and that He had someone perfectly suited for me, one who would be faithful. We would serve Him together.

God, did you cause the mailperson to be early that day, so I couldn't mail the wedding invitations?

Yes, and I will continue to open and close doors for you so that you will walk in all my ways, [Proverbs 3:5–6]. I will heal your heart, and I will be the one to join you to the man I need you to be with for your faith journey. The words seemed to resonate in my inner being.

I cancelled all the wedding arrangements I had made and continued pursuing my university degree, all while waiting upon God to mend my heart and wondering who God would bring to me.

Unbeknownst to me, while God was preparing me, he was also preparing Rick, the man I would one day meet and marry.

Rick also was engaged to be married to someone else, but God had been stirring reservations inside him, making him feel he should not marry her. Rick would later say his love for her overshadowed his heart's reservations from the Lord.

Three days before their planned elopement, Rick had to return home from college for an uncle's funeral. On the funeral morning, he told his family he and his fiancé were going to another state to be married by a justice of the peace. His parents were in shock. Although they had met the woman and knew she was divorced with a child, they didn't know her well. And regardless of who he married, they wanted their son and fiancé to have a Christian church wedding rather than eloping.

I waited for God to show me beyond a doubt that He had opened the door for this relationship.

Before returning to college, Rick asked to take his brother's new motorcycle out for a short ride before his drive back to school. His brother tossed him the keys. Thirty minutes later, he wrapped the motorcycle and himself around an electric pole. He lay in a ditch along a back country road for some time—long enough for him to be afraid that he would die there—before a good Samaritan came along and found him. At the hospital, tests revealed a three-inch compound fracture in his right femur. The internal injuries required several days to stabilize before the leg surgery could commence.

After surgery, they told him he might not walk normally again. He had a month-long hospital stay, followed by several months of recovery in his parents' home. Rick would later say, "God had blocked my way so I could not move. He plunged my path into darkness."

A couple of months into his recovery, Rick rededicated his life to Jesus. His fiancé called the very night of his rededication to tell him the wedding was off. That day, a miracle healing began. Soon he was able to walk and run without any pain or limp, making it possible to remove the fourteen-inch rod from his leg.

A year later, we met at church and eventually began dating. Rick knew before I did that God wanted us to be married. I was slow to commit to another marriage proposal because I had been so sure my first fiancé was the one for me that I was afraid to trust my feelings again. It was only later that I realized I hadn't inquired of the Lord what He thought, and I decided I wouldn't make that mistake again. So, I waited for God to show me beyond a doubt that He had opened the door for this relationship.

Several months into dating, Rick would tell me he loved me, and I would smile and say "I like you a lot. But I won't let go of my heart until God lets me know that you are truly the one He told me about."

Then one night, I had a dream. In the dream, Rick and I were leaving church after a young adult meeting, holding hands as we walked to my car. Rick opened the door, and I got in. In the dream I rolled down my window, and Rick leaned in to tell me what he usually said, "I love you." But in the dream, he added, "I will wait until you know."

Weeks went by and I forgot about the dream. Then one Wednesday night, as we were walking out of church after a young adult meeting and holding hands, I vaguely felt that I had lived this event before. I didn't connect it to the dream until Rick opened the door and I rolled down the window.

Was this the moment God had showed me? I knew that if he said those extra words, the ones he'd never said before, it was the "yes" from God I was waiting for.

"I love you," Rick told me that night. "I will wait until you know."

I leaned out and kissed him. "I love you too!" Poor Rick almost fainted.

We can make plans, but sometimes God must step in and take us in another direction so that we can fulfill our destinies.

Today, Rick and I serve together as associate pastors, and as I write this we have been married for fifty-two years.

God Knows Our Need Before We Do

Sylvia Schroeder

This service that you perform is not only supplying the needs of the Lord's people but is also overflowing in many expressions of thanks to God.

—2 CORINTHIANS 9:12 (NIV)

I awoke with a start, unsure what had pulled me from sleep. The only sound seemed to be the wild beating of my own heart, its thump so loud that my ears dulled to every other sound. The telephone trilled into the silence, shattering the stillness. Startled, I swung my feet out of bed and ran toward the noise.

It was a middle-of-the-night, across-the-ocean-call. The kind I dreaded. By the time I'd reached the phone, I'd already listed in my mind all the horrible things that could have happened, and worried about what I could do across the seven time zones of distance that separated me from my children.

My husband and I served in foreign missions. Our children grew up in other cultures, learning other languages. Those years spent in global Christian ministry led to many wonderful experiences, but also many tearful goodbyes. And when our children got older and went on to colleges and new lives across oceans, I worried about their safety. I prayed hard for them. And to be honest, my worried prayers held doubt and a decided lack of trust. Inside I felt a constant panic, as if I needed to pray just right, often enough, or with sufficient fervor for God to hear me. And, at times I felt like His own presence was an ocean away.

Tonight, though, my daughter Charity wasn't calling with an emergency, but with a story that had astounded her so much she couldn't wait to share.

Dread coursed through her like an electric shock when she glanced down at the gas gauge. Her tank was empty.

"Oh Mom." Charity's excited voice carried through the long-distance connection. "You're not going to believe what happened."

Currently living in Delaware, Charity filled her newly married days with running from one job to another and then to class. After working the morning preschool teaching shift, she went to her second job at the church's afternoon day care. That day when my phone rang in the middle of my night, she'd had an exceptionally tiring morning.

"I just knew I would be late to class," Charity's voice recounted over the miles that separated us, "so I ran to the van 'cause I needed to hurry."

The old clunky blue van had been given to them by a friend. With books tucked under one arm and her purse hanging off the other, she fitted the key into the door, wiggled it just right, and yanked it open. Slinging her purse and books inside, she climbed into the driver's seat. The heavy door screeched in protest as she pulled it hard, slammed it shut, and turned the ignition.

The parking lot was almost empty. Parents had picked up their little ones and everyone had already gone home. The van was making strange noises, shaking and thumping. Charity bent forward, straining to hear the insides of the old car with its wheezing and belching. Tin can vibrations rattled her seat as the van shimmied, shook, and backfired.

We can't afford car problems, Charity thought while she sat and waited, hoping it would begin running smoothly. "Come on, come on," she coaxed. "I've got to get to class."

Not really paying attention to anything but the car, she jumped about a foot when someone knocked on the window. Her big blue eyes were round like saucers, her hand smacked flat against her racing heart, and she gulped for breath.

Outside the car door, at eye level a coworker's smiling face greeted her. "Charity!" her fellow teacher shouted above the ungainly sputtering of the engine.

Charity didn't know what to do. *I can't talk to anyone now,* she thought. *I'm going to be late.* Hoping she could get away with a smile and a wave, she was getting ready to start rolling away when she saw that the older woman was waving her arm, holding something in her fist.

Charity stopped and cranked down the window. The sun was low and so bright it silhouetted the woman outside, the autumn air wafting into the car. She squinted at the woman through the half-open window, forcing a smile as an uncomfortable feeling churned in her gut.

"I don't know why," the older woman said, "but God just pressed it on my heart to give this to you." The preschool teacher thrust her arm into the half-opened window and opened her tightly closed fist. Green dollar bills danced in the breeze. She curled her hand around them again and pressed the bills toward Charity. "I feel like God is telling me I should give this to you."

The unexpectedness of it made Charity stutter. "Oh, uh, no thanks, I mean . . ." Uneasy and unsure how to react, she tried to refuse. "Thank you, but I really don't need it."

"But I really think God wants me to give it to you," the lady insisted again. "It's not a lot, twenty dollars is all."

Surprised, perhaps a little embarrassed, and most definitely in a hurry, Charity finally took the offered money. She shoved it into her empty purse and drove off with a smile and a wave to plunge into the thick stream of cars in rush-hour traffic.

As she navigated onto the freeway and headed toward the community college, the car hiccupped. Dread coursed through her like an electric shock when she glanced down at the gas gauge. Her tank was empty.

The older teacher's words from the parking lot echoed in Charity's memory: "I don't know why, but God just pressed it on my heart to give this to you."

Charity had not remembered to check the gas gauge, and had no money in her purse except what the lady had handed her. She knew God had indeed sent her coworker to provide what she didn't even know she needed.

An exit ahead took her rolling into a gas station. She would not have made it to another.

As I listened to Charity's story, we shared a giggle over the visual of her jumping in shock when the other teacher knocked on the window and joked about her attempt to avoid getting bogged down in a conversation. But as her story unfolded in the quiet night, I began to recognize God in the details, His provision and protection standing against my own constant worry. How like God to give my newlywed daughter in a clunker van with no gas nor money, a reminder of His continual presence even before she knew she needed it.

Neither my daughter nor I had any way of knowing that those brief moments would be ones we would remember and cherish in years to come.

A few years later, a brain stem lesion robbed Charity of mobility and communication. For almost two years, she lingered between life and death. The intense trial called for all of us who loved her to pull from a storehouse of faith that affirmed His constant presence, reminding us He knows our needs even before we do.

Today she testifies of God's presence and faithfulness from the constraints of a power chair. She still remembers that day in the parking lot, a sweet reminder of God's constant care for His beloved children. It's something she's carried all through her life, helping prepare her for its darkest moments.

But perhaps I learned an even bigger lesson from that night long ago when my daughter woke me from the dead of night with a phone call.

How like our loving heavenly Father to provide something so small yet so tangible as twenty dollars to show me, living an ocean away in my own sea of anxiety, that He knows my children's needs even before they do. He is present when they make mistakes or are forgetful. He is a God who sees the sparrow fall, and clothes the lilies of the fields. He takes note of gas gauges, and He surely watches over His children.

"God told me to give this to you," Charity repeated with wonder that night on the phone. "Mom, have you ever had anything like that happen to you?"

"I just did," I answered.

I remember and am humbled by the personal way God cares for us. We may be physically distant from one another, but we are never far from God. We are held in His love.

A Mother's Advice Brought Blessings All Around

Lynette Blair Mitchell

⟿⟿———————○———————⟿⟿

A generous person will prosper; whoever
refreshes others will be refreshed.

—Proverbs 11:25 (niv)

Years ago, in a therapy session for cancer survivors, I heard for the first time the phrase "the lion in the closet." The group moderator explained that anyone who has been diagnosed with and treated for cancer lives constantly with the fear of the dreaded disease returning, hence "the lion in the closet."

One dreary morning, as rain cascaded down by the gallon, the lion in my closet was roaring. I had battled breast cancer almost twelve years earlier and had had no evidence of disease for more than a decade. But a recent ultrasound of my thyroid showed a pesky nodule that might need further investigation. My primary doctor wanted it to be biopsied. I was horrified.

I had worked so hard to stay out of cancer's way since my initial diagnosis. I had my left breast removed, received chemotherapy, and underwent blistering radiation. Then I changed my diet, exercised more, and prayed like never before. I diligently took pills for ten years to prevent recurrence.

And yet, here I was in utter angst. I reached out to the throat oncologist who had been monitoring my thyroid for years, but he couldn't see me for two weeks. That dreaded lion began banging on the closet door and rattling the doorknob. I tearfully told my nearly 80-year-old mother. But my tough-as-nails mama doesn't let anybody sit on the pity pot for long. "Get your mind off yourself," she said. "Go do something for somebody else."

With the sky slate gray and my mood even darker, I took my mama's advice and sat with the Lord. I simply asked, "God, who can I bless today? I'm tired of being afraid. I know You are a healer, and my life is in Your hands. I know You don't want me sitting here moping about my problems. Let me do Your will today."

As with Elijah, the Lord didn't shout His answer. He simply whispered in my heart: *Get the chicken.*

I knew exactly what He meant.

Months earlier, a dear friend of mine was diagnosed with multiple myeloma. I had taken some food and gift cards to bless her at the time. She mentioned that her husband liked a particular grocery store's fried chicken, but I had never gotten around to getting it for him.

Now my friend was still pretty much homebound, staying clear of excessive public contact as her immune system rebounded from a stem cell transplant. After my prayer, I knew the Lord wanted me to get up and get the fried chicken to my friend.

The decision to obey was the easy part. Carrying out the good deed tested my resolve.

I wanted to get the chicken to my friend's house by early afternoon at the latest so I wouldn't get caught in the pouring rain *and* late afternoon traffic. It seemed that the forces designed to derail me got busy as soon as the thought crossed my mind.

Obstacle number one: I called the grocery store and was told that the chicken was out of stock and that the delivery truck wouldn't arrive until early afternoon. That pushed my pickup time to mid-afternoon, with at least a half-hour drive to my friend's home afterward. I would be flirting with commuter traffic the entire time I drove between our two zip codes.

I sighed and rearranged my morning, making my way to the store right after lunch. As I pulled into the parking lot, obstacle number two stopped me in my tracks: I got a text alerting me that one of my employees had turned in her two-week notice. I was already short staffed, so I spent thirty minutes sitting in my car with the windshield wipers furiously whisking back and forth, trying to convince that employee to reconsider. When she refused despite my efforts, I was deflated, and I wanted to leave my call-ahead chicken order in the store and go back home. After all, I rationalized, my friend did not know about my plans to provide her with a meal.

But again, I heard the command from the core of my being: *Get the chicken.*

I ended my work call and stomped through sloshy puddles to get inside the store. Obstacle number three met me at the deli counter: A woman with a hair net securely affixed on her head told me my chicken order was not ready. Smiling kindly, she said she needed another fifteen minutes. Now, I was no longer flirting with traffic—it was a definite date!

I tried to smile back. As I waited, I aimlessly steered my cart toward the snacks aisle and grabbed junk food I didn't need. Thirty minutes later, I was finally back in my car with a bucket of fresh, hot chicken—and a couple of bags of chips. My schedule was already shot to smithereens, so I stopped by a popular sandwich shop and got hot soup and a large Caesar salad to round out the chicken meal.

I heard the command from the core of my being: Get the chicken.

When I finally pulled into my friend's driveway, half the day was gone. I opened my car door to retrieve all the food, and the plastic shopping bag holding the chicken bucket attempted to fall onto the soggy ground. I grabbed it before a potential obstacle number four could completely upend all my efforts. "Oh, no you don't," I growled at the cooked bird.

Feeling triumphantly resilient, I skipped up the steps to my friend's porch and rang the bell. She answered the door with delighted surprise, thinking that I had just come for a visit. But when I shoved the bag forward and told her I had come with the scrumptious fried chicken, she threw her head back and began to laugh.

I couldn't imagine what was so funny. My damp appearance, perhaps? I was so confused.

"Lynette, we've been trying to get some of this chicken for two days," she explained. "We went Saturday, and they were sold out. We went yesterday and the line was so long that we gave up. And here you come today with the chicken. Girl, come on in!"

My friend and I sat in her family room and marveled over the omniscience and greatness of our God. When I put my big worry into His caring, capable hands, He orchestrated events to satisfy a simple desire of my friend's heart.

As I drove home, I didn't even notice the traffic I had so desperately tried to avoid. I was so consumed with gratitude. God had chosen grumpy ole me to be a part of His greater plan. I was so thankful that He gently encouraged me to stay the course and be obedient when I wanted to give up.

When my day finally ended, the biggest revelation and gift from God dawned on me: The lion in the closet was no longer roaring.

God's Mysterious Ways: Being a Blessing to Others

Have you ever been so overwhelmed with your own issues that you miss God's prompting to be a blessing to someone else? Instead of wallowing in our own mess—the problems, the worries, the cares that can fill our days—what if we allowed God to show us someone who needed us? As you'll read in many stories throughout this book, serving others can lift our own hearts along with the other person's.

- ❧ **Pray.** When you find yourself sitting in your circumstances, wondering how God is going to show up, ask Him to show you how you can show up for someone else, be an answer to *their* prayer.

- ❧ **Seek.** The Bible instructs us to bear each other's burdens. Without minimizing your own grief or pain or concerns, seek out ways you can bless others. And be sure to let others be a blessing to you when you're in need. Blessings don't flow just one way.

- ❧ **Act.** Sometimes being a blessing to others just looks like giving them a call to see how they're doing. Do you have a friend who's been going through a hard time? Set aside thirty minutes to talk on the phone with them, lifting thom up in prayer and reminding them they are seen and heard.

- ❧ **Reflect.** What does it mean to love your neighbor as yourself? How have you been letting others love you? How can you show love to others?

Every Child Counts

By Amy Flynn-Smith, as told to Stephanie Thompson

---

*Pure and undefiled religion before God and the Father
is this: to visit orphans and widows in their trouble,
and to keep oneself unspotted from the world.*

—JAMES 1:27 (NKJV)

I took a deep breath and plopped into a chair at the kitchen table. My three-year-old and four-year-old sons played upstairs. Soon, my three other children would be home from school. Finally, a moment to myself to reflect and pray. That's when the strangest thought came into my mind: *There's a child in China who needs you.*

A child in China needs me? I had five biological children right here who needed me! But the urge was undeniable—an overwhelming feeling that we were supposed to adopt a baby.

True, I loved kids, but I was quite content being a stay-at-home mom to five of them. I had no problem getting pregnant, so the notion of adopting had not crossed my mind. But instead of going away, the idea grew stronger. Every time I prayed, I would have an overwhelming impression that a little girl in an orphanage, halfway across the world in China, was meant to join our family.

After a few weeks my husband warmed to the idea, and we began international adoption proceedings. A year later, my twelve-year-old daughter and I boarded an airplane to China. The orphanage caregivers brought our beautiful baby girl from the town of Shantou to our hotel room. She was so tiny and weak from living in a crowded institution. A sense of overwhelming love enveloped me as I cradled this precious eight-month-old in my arms. We named her Anna.

I discovered that as a newborn, Anna had been left in a straw basket on a village sidewalk in the early hours of the morning—no note, no explanation.

From her first days, I explained to Anna how she came to be in our family. Anna went from babydom to toddlerhood to a preschooler hearing about her adoption. "You were born in China to a woman we will always honor because she gave you life," I'd begin the familiar story.

Once Anna started talking, she had questions beyond her years. She wanted to know who took care of her in China. What her life was like. Why her parents didn't raise her. One evening as I sat on the side of the tub while Anna took a bath, she looked at me with her beautiful brown eyes and asked, "Do you think they loved me?" I knew immediately my three-year-old daughter was thinking about the circumstances surrounding her birth. I wanted to help her get answers.

It took months, but I finally received permission to visit her orphanage. In January 2003, the taxi stopped in front of a six-story building with the words *Children's Paradise* above the front door. I waved to tiny faces who peered through metal bars on upstairs windows as an interpreter and I got out of the car.

Stepping inside, the stock-stillness was unexpected. I knew hundreds of children lived here, so the unnatural silence pierced my heart immediately. I followed a nanny—the same one who had brought Anna to our hotel room three years earlier—upstairs. We walked past row after row of metal baby cribs filled with abandoned children. They stared solemnly at me, but never made a sound. That natural instinct to communicate their needs, the cries or whines my own children used to get my attention before they could speak, didn't exist here. They had sadly learned that their cries for help would not be answered.

Time seemed to move in slow motion as my mind struggled to grasp that all of these children were orphaned. We entered a baby room that was cold, but clean, with spartan conditions. Rows of infants bundled in threadbare snowsuits and blankets lay flat on their backs on top of straw mats in the cribs. Their little cheeks were red and chapped from the winter air, as this orphanage, like most in China, didn't have a heating system. Even though I was in a southern city, it was extremely cold.

A staff member pointed to a blue metal crib and indicated Anna had slept there. Emotions overwhelmed me as I pictured my precocious, vivacious daughter in this eerily quiet room. I discovered that as a newborn, Anna had been left in a straw basket on a village sidewalk in the early hours of the morning—no note, no explanation. She was found by police and brought here. As I looked at the infant who'd replaced her in the crib, my tears flowed freely.

On the next floor was the toddler room. Children sat at miniature tables waiting for their first of only two meals that day—white rice in metal bowls. One extremely thin girl caught my attention as she scraped the sides of the bowl trying to get every grain. I knelt to her level and noticed her lips and hands were deep blue. I gently took her hand in mine. Her fingers were like ice.

The next morning, I lamented to the Lord. Was I nuts to attempt this?

I asked the nannies if I could share some pork jerky I'd bought from a street vendor on the way to the orphanage. When the bag was pulled out, every eye in the room was locked onto it. I ripped off a small amount and gave it to the child. When the others saw the meat, their mouths dropped open like baby birds. I slowly walked from child to child, hand feeding each one, as they slowly savored the morsels. It was all I could do not to melt in a puddle of tears.

Later that morning, the staff doctor greeted me. We walked to the crib of a baby boy whose skin was dark blue. He pointed to the child's heart and shook his head sadly. I realized then that the little boy, who was struggling to breathe, had been born with a heart defect. I naively asked when his surgery would be, only to be told the funds were not available to save nine-month-old Kang's life. As I reached into the crib and cradled the baby, the child who would die without medical intervention, I felt as if my own heart would break in two.

Once I returned to the States, I shared with Anna about the orphanage where she had lived and the nannies who had cared for her. I tried everything in my power to get back to life as usual. It was impossible to sleep after what I'd seen; I couldn't shake the heavy hopelessness I felt for those children. There was only one cure for my blanket of sorrow—I had to act. I knew I couldn't help every orphan in China, but maybe I could help one little boy whose heart was failing.

I composed an email about the overwhelming need at the orphanage and sent it to everyone on my contact list. I asked people to pray, tell others, and send donations to fund Kang's life-saving surgery. Emails from complete strangers flooded my inbox. Checks, letters, and pledges trickled in from generous friends and adoptive parents. I learned a pediatric heart surgeon in Denver had scheduled a medical mission to China next month. He agreed to operate on Kang and asked me to contact the orphanage for the baby's medical records. He donated his skills, but the hospital, nursing staff, and medications would need to be paid up front. The total needed was $5,000.

My shoulders dropped. I'd never been comfortable asking people for money. When my kids had school fundraisers, I'd just as soon write a check than ask friends or neighbors to buy something. A few hundred dollars had come in from my email, but raising several thousand seemed out of reach.

Gaining my composure, I emailed the orphanage about the upcoming opportunity with the heart surgeon and asked for Kang's medical records. I quickly received his records, along with the files of two additional children in their care who needed heart surgery as well, including the little girl on the toddler floor who prompted me to share my jerky. But I wasn't close to funding even the first surgery. Adding to my discouragement, more than one friend voiced opinions that we should prioritize helping those within our own borders instead of orphans in China.

I tripled my efforts, calling and emailing everyone I knew. I asked friends of friends to forward my requests. The checks poured in.

The next morning, I lamented to the Lord. Was I nuts to attempt this? Or worse, was I wrong to offer help to dying kids overseas? Tears dripped down my cheeks, and I heard three simple words spoken to my heart—words spoken by the Lord: *every child counts.*

I sat quietly and let the weight of those words settle deep inside my soul. Not just those in the US or those fortunate enough to be born healthy, but every child who entered this world, regardless of location, circumstances or special needs, counted in the eyes of God.

I tripled my efforts, calling and emailing everyone I knew. I asked friends of friends to forward my requests. The checks poured in. Some $5, some $100, and one generous person who had been praying on how to spend a year-end bonus sent $5,000. In three short weeks, God provided enough money through these people to fund all the surgeries and related expenses. The children were moved to the hospital the very next week.

Not only were all three heart procedures successful, but they also allowed these children to become healthy enough for adoption. Our original goal, of course, was to save their lives, but doesn't every child deserve a home with loving parents?

As news of the surgeries spread, other orphanages began emailing me about children in need of medical help. Adoptive parents and medical professionals across the US began eagerly volunteering their time and talents to help these kids in need.

That summer, four of us moms and a nurse filed incorporation papers to create a registered charity dedicated to providing hope and healing to orphaned children—Love Without Boundaries. Our name was inspired by a flag given to me from the Chinese government after that first heart surgery trip, with the words: Love Makes No Boundaries Between Countries.

I couldn't help but marvel at what God was doing! I watched our foundation grow from providing a handful of heart surgeries in 2003 to touching the lives of more than 150,000 children through life-saving surgeries and cleft lip repairs, supplying formula and hot meals, medical supplies, warm blankets, safe cribs, establishing local foster care programs, and building schools. At one point, Love Without Boundaries was the second-largest orphan charity in China, working in almost every province.

In 2016, Love Without Boundaries decided to "live out our name" and expand into a worldwide effort. Today, children in 21 countries like Cambodia, Guatemala, India, and Uganda have received our services. In each country, we partner with local experts to address the core needs of children in their community. All our services are united under the belief that every child, regardless of their needs, circumstances, or location, deserves to know love.

Twenty-five years have passed since God whispered to my heart that a child in China needed me. I'll never cease to be amazed how a child's deep questions about her early life and orphanage sparked a global mission. A child in China needed me? God showed me that children across the world need all of us to step up when they are hurting. I'm so grateful He taught me such a powerful truth—*every* child counts.

Balancing Act

Terrie Todd

If any of you lacks wisdom, you should ask God,
who gives generously to all without finding fault,
and it will be given to you.

—James 1:5 (NIV)

L *ord, please help me be a blessing to the people around*
me today, whether friends or strangers. Grant me wis-
dom and opportunities to encourage others. Give me
words to say that surpass my own limited understanding.

I looked at the words I'd written in my prayer journal, then closed it to hurry off to breakfast and begin day two of the Christian writers' conference I was attending. Would God grant me the opportunity I'd prayed for?

In our morning session, one of our major exercises was learning how to create a "writer's manifesto." The facilitator explained how writing our own manifestos can help writers define our identity, unify our goals, stay excited and moti-vated, keep focused, and improve our understanding. She had us begin by studying a list of 150 words that could be consid-ered values. We circled the words that resonated with us most, trying to keep it to fifty or fewer.

Next, we reduced our list of values to twenty-five and wrote each of these words on a separate slip of paper. The next step was separating these slips into three piles: *always, sometimes,* and *infrequently.* That completed, we were instructed to keep only the *always* pile and "kick the others to the curb," no matter how precious they seemed. Then, arranging those *always* values in order of importance, we narrowed them down to our top seven. This difficult but worthwhile exercise was designed to reveal what we truly, deeply valued.

From there, we drafted our manifestos on large sheets of paper. After working on that for a while, participants paired off to show each other our progress. We were given a limited amount of time to explain the manifesto to our partner and to receive their feedback before reversing turns.

My partner was a lovely lady named Linda, whom I'd met that morning. I knew only her first name, that she was married, that she was local and not staying overnight at the conference venue, and that she would be running home to walk her dog between the afternoon and evening sessions. That's all.

Yet, when she began showing me her manifesto-in-progress, one of her value words jumped out at me: *balance.* Although it was one of the words on the list and is something most of us constantly strive for, I somehow got the distinct impression that this word belonged in the "kick it to the curb" pile—at least for Linda. How could I possibly know that, though? This woman was a stranger. Should I say what I thought? Doing so seemed awfully bold. Could I risk hurting her with such an audacious suggestion? Was this a nudge from God or simply my own limited understanding?

The concept of balance had strong personal associations for me. At one point in my life, I was raising three children while juggling three part-time jobs and three college courses. Friends often asked me how I managed to keep life "in balance." In truth, life always felt off-kilter and still does. Perhaps that's what caused me to draw the conclusion that balance is an illusion. It's not biblical. Ever since sin entered the world, everything has been out of whack. Nothing is the way God intended, so why do we think we somehow hold the power to bring our lives into balance? God alone can step in and make things right. Our job is to follow.

Could I risk hurting her with such an audacious suggestion? Was this a nudge from God or simply my own limited understanding?

These were some of the thoughts swirling in my brain as I listened to my new friend. Almost before I knew it, I heard words coming from my mouth. "Linda," I said. "I could be wrong here, but I'm wondering if the word *balance* belongs on your manifesto. I know we put a lot of stock into leading balanced lives, but I'm not sure it's realistic. Sometimes we place way too much pressure on ourselves to achieve something that might not even be possible—at least not in the way we might view it."

Her eyes welled up. *Oh no. Have I hurt her feelings?*

She invited me to say more.

I shared with her something I'd learned from my church. Years before, realizing our own limitations in this area, we'd begun a three-week cycle that we called "Upside Down." It was based on Acts 17:6, where the followers of Jesus are described as "these that have turned the world upside down" (KJV). On our *up* weeks, we focused attention on our relationship with God in our worship, receiving of communion, and teaching. On *side* weeks, we emphasized our relationships with each other as brothers and sisters in Christ by taking more time for fellowship. On *down* weeks, we concentrated on metaphorically kneeling to serve our community in humble acts of service.

After some time using this cycle to keep our faith practices in balance, our leadership realized an important component was still missing: celebration. Now, we run on a four-week cycle, calling the fourth week *party* week. We hear stories of all the good things God is doing in our midst, spend extra time in praise and worship, and share a potluck lunch.

All these facets of faith life need to be kept in balance, but trying to do all of them all the time is unrealistic. A visitor to our church on any given week might easily draw the conclusion that we're horribly off-balance, placing all our energy into only one component. By focusing on one each week and rotating them consistently, we've done much better at the whole concept of balance. Through that example, I learned that different seasons of life call for me to lean hard in one direction while allowing others to slide for a time.

"That's exactly what I needed to hear," Linda said. I hoped to hear more, but the workshop facilitator called the group back to order. She invited us to share with the larger group what insights we'd gained by giving and receiving feedback. Linda surprised me by raising her hand. "My partner gave me some wise words I really needed today," she told the others without elaborating.

Though I'll probably never learn the details of Linda's life, I felt truly humbled and grateful, knowing God had guided me in this. Only later did I recall what I'd written in my prayer journal that morning. Why had I been so surprised when God answered my prayer, partnering me with someone who needed to be lifted up and then giving me just the right words to say?

When you walk daily with the Lord, He gives you a good heart and blesses you with wisdom when you ask. Trust Him to do what He says He will do.

A God-Given Number

Stacey Thureen

But you, dear friends, by building yourselves up in your most holy faith and praying in the Holy Spirit, keep yourselves in God's love as you wait for the mercy of our Lord Jesus Christ to bring you to eternal life.

—JUDE 1:20–21 (NIV)

Nearly 100 swimmers were divided up into five small groups. When we heard the signal to start, we left the shoreline gracefully in a cascade of freestyle strokes and flutter kicks. The calm swooshing sound of water surrounded me. Adrenaline was rushing through my body as if I'd drunk a large cup of caffeinated coffee, keeping me awake for the long duration of the early morning race.

The sun's rays were shining down onto the relatively calm water of Square Lake in Stillwater, Minnesota. This was not only my first time ever swimming an open-water 5K, but also my first time swimming in an open-water event without wearing a wetsuit to provide extra buoyance and warmth. Thankfully, the water temperature was ideal for that time of the year. Still, as a safety precaution, there was a buoy attached to me by a belt around my waist, dragging its way through the water behind me.

This endurance race was exhausting and exhilarating at the same time. As I swam, I reminded myself to focus on my breath pattern. To make sure I was still swimming straight, I'd pick my head up to "spot" where I was, then put my head down and keep going if I didn't need to correct or reposition my body in the water.

Keep going, I told myself. *You can do this!*

As I rounded the last big buoy, I could see the straight-away leading to the giant red inflatable finish sign. As I tried to increase my arm turnover and kicking pace and pick up my head to see where I was going, I could see the red inflatable getting bigger and bigger. To my right, I saw a couple of other swimmers getting closer to me. I tried with all my might to just keep swimming—and then I was across the line.

There it was again—121. I began to wonder if God was trying to tell me something.

As I approached the shore, I was careful to not stand up out of the water too quickly, a transition that had made me dizzy at the end of past open-water swims. This time it happened again. Recovering, I walked around, grabbed something to cover myself with because I felt cold, ate a snack, and drank some water. It took my body time to warm up, but my spirits brightened when I saw my coach and friend, John Jacobson—who had also participated in the race—swimming toward the finish line.

"Way to go, John! You did great!"

"How did you do?" he asked right away.

"I came in second in my age group and tenth overall among men and women. My time was one hour and twenty-one minutes."

At the time, I didn't realize the significance that number would take on during the summer open-water swimming season and beyond.

Four weeks later, my husband and I traveled to Pierre, South Dakota, the host site for the 2023 United States Masters Swimming Middle-Distance Open-Water Nationals. The location was the Oahe Dam on the Missouri River. This 2.25-mile straight swim was nestled at the edge of a rocky earthen dam.

The morning of the swim, all the participants congregated to check-in and have numbers written on their arms with a black permanent marker.

"Your race number is 121."

That day, I didn't need to wear a special buoy or wetsuit. The swim began at the west side of the dam near the boat ramps. The course followed the shoreline of the dam moving east towards the intakes. There were three large groups of swimmers, staggered ten minutes apart from each other. The conditions were just perfect. There was no South Dakota wind wiping across the water, and the sun was beating down on the water, giving us a nice temperature and clear view for the morning swim.

I finished as the fastest female swimmer, winning my age group and receiving National Champion and All-American honors. I noticed that I had paced one minute and twenty-one seconds per 100 meters. There it was again—121.

I began to wonder if God was trying to tell me something.

In the weeks to come, I read and meditated on Psalm 121, which begins: "I lift up my eyes to the mountains—where does my help come from? My help comes from the LORD, the Maker of heaven and earth" (NIV). The words written in it were exactly what I needed. Words of hope and encouragement. A reminder that God is with me, He is for me. A reminder that the Lord watches over me and protects me, helping me no matter what I'm going through.

Weeks later, God used this psalm to help me overcome a big fear. I had been struggling with performance anxiety around swimming my best event from high school and college: the 200-meter butterfly. I held onto each word in the psalm. With the wisdom of Scripture and guidance from John, God helped me trust Him and swim this event.

When I finished, I didn't look over my shoulder to glance at the scoreboard to see my time. I had just wanted to swim the race without focusing on the outcome. As I was warming down, John came over to talk to me.

"Stacey, the official said you swam a 2:42.09."

As soon as what he said sank in, I was awed by seeing God at work. "John you know what my time is, right?"

"What?"

"That's one minute and twenty-one seconds—multiplied by two!"

We both laughed with joy. We couldn't believe it. God had helped me swim an event I feared so much and even gave me a time that fit with the God-given number 121.

The time from that swim meet sparked an interest in me to read the chapter one, verse twenty-ones found throughout the books of the Bible. Not every book in the Bible has a 1:21, but those that did spoke to me. Many of the recurring themes had to do with creation; God's will to produce; God's desire for His children to humble themselves, to persevere, and to wait on Him. It seemed like God was creating a personal reading plan to strengthen my faith. I shared some of these things with my husband, Kyle, and with John, who knew about how God kept giving me 121. It also inspired him to read Psalm 121 and other 1:21 verses.

Months after that swim, I was on my way home from dropping my youngest daughter off at preschool. I turned on the local Christian radio station in the van. What was normally an eight-minute drive to our house became a lot longer due to a train crossing. As I waited in traffic, less than one mile from home, I heard the radio host announce that he was going to read Psalm 121.

"This is a psalm about someone who is journeying," he said.

As the radio announcer read with conviction in his voice, he placed such an emphasis on each verse. The enthusiastic and warm tone of his voice helped me understand the importance of the words in a way I hadn't before. After hearing it read out loud in the van, I felt lifted by God's Word as I read through Psalm 121 that afternoon.

Most importantly, I felt encouraged to keep reading Scripture. In the weeks prior to God giving me the number 121, I hadn't been keeping up with reading the Bible. While I was still doing daily readings, I was far behind in my reading plan and trying to catch up. Now I understood that God was giving me this personal reading plan to help revitalize and strengthen my faith, and to help me share that with others. No matter how enjoyable—or sometimes mundane—reading the Bible can be, I can trust that in all seasons of life God has a good plan. I will stay committed to reading His Word.

Job Advancement

Mary Portzen

*"The LORD himself goes before you and will be
with you; he will never leave you nor forsake you.
Do not be afraid; do not be discouraged."*

—DEUTERONOMY 31:8 (NIV)

I loved my job. Or at least, I loved the position I'd been hired
for in 2018, working as a program coordinator at a spirituality center. My job was to plan and implement programs that
would reach a new audience in the local community, where the
previous core audience had been an aging population of nuns.

The road to get to my current position had been full of
twists and turns. When my husband died in 2012, I'd spent
the previous thirty years as a stay-at-home mom and had
no job experience outside of freelance writing and running
various home businesses. I still managed to land a part-time
position as the director of a small-town library and also began
to conduct writing workshops for other libraries and community colleges. After the loss of my husband, mother, and
grandson in quick succession, I felt God lead me to become
a grief counselor, which then helped me start an annual grief
retreat. I had seven books published in eight years, and those
books helped me get a job as a newspaper reporter.

I had no doubt the cumulation of these jobs and experiences, coupled with a long-ago college degree in psychology, prepared me for the job at the spirituality center. It was a dream come true, a workplace where I could talk about faith and pray with co-workers. I thrived in my position, developing programs on creativity and grief, two topics I was passionate about. Community residents who'd never before set foot in a spirituality center attended them. Every morning, I woke up excited, wondering how God would use me that day.

On a Sunday afternoon my husband and I held hands and prayed together, asking God to make it clear if He wanted me to leave my job.

By the summer of 2021, well established as an author and speaker, I'd founded an annual grief retreat and writer's conference and was earning a hefty salary. By the world's standards, I was a "success," something that was important to me when I met Nick, a long-time owner of a bowling center who'd been widowed three years before. I never wanted him to think it was his own apparent success that had attracted me.

Ours was a whirlwind courtship, one that involved prayer from the beginning. Convinced God had brought us together, we got married six weeks after we met. My youngest daughter rented my house, and Nick sold his. We moved to an apartment in the town where I worked, an hour from his business. The arrangement made sense. Nick's grandson had taken over the bulk of the management of his business, while my boss allowed me to rearrange my schedule to fit around my husband's hours.

It seemed that God had brought me to a perfect place in my life, one that balanced a loving home life with work that was deeply fulfilling. It was with some consternation that I realized, not long after my marriage to Nick, that the leadership team at the spirituality center was planning major changes to our programming. At least I suspected as much when my boss called me into her office to ask how I'd feel if I was someday asked to give up the writing, art, and grief-related programs I'd been conducting.

"I wouldn't want to stay," I admitted. The idea of giving up the programs I'd been hired for, that brought me so much joy, seemed preposterous. "The only thing worse would be if I had to do programs on agriculture."

We both laughed at the incongruity of the idea. My boss knew that agriculture had been my least favorite subject to cover in my former job as a reporter.

The next day the team leader called us into a meeting.

"We have some ideas for programming we want to run by you. A lot of our nuns grew up on farms, and they're asking for more programs centered around agriculture."

My eyes widened. I looked across the table where my boss sat. Her mouth hung open, her eyes signaling the same shock I felt.

"Mary, what is happening?" she asked as we headed back to our offices. "Why would they say the exact same thing you'd mentioned?"

I just shook my head. I didn't tell her that as soon as the word *agriculture* was spoken, I'd heard something else, a clear message from the Holy Spirit.

You don't belong here.

I wrestled with those words for days, uncertain what they meant. Surely God wasn't asking me to leave such a perfect job? That didn't make sense! I'd never made so much money or had such generous benefits. But I knew what I'd heard.

Nick, not about to sway me one way or the other, suggested we pray about it. On a Sunday afternoon we held hands and prayed together, asking God to make it clear if He wanted me to leave my job.

"This week," I added boldly. "Make it clear this week."

The following morning, one of the women on the leadership team stopped at my office.

"You've been concentrating a lot on creativity and grief since you were hired," she commented. "We'd like to see that change. We have some ideas besides the agriculture theme." She mentioned several topics that didn't interest me in the least. I gulped. Was this God's answer?

When I told Nick about the conversation, he encouraged me to continue praying. "God will show you what to do," he insisted.

On Wednesday I got a call from a nun who'd attended many of my events.

"Have you thought about doing fewer creativity and grief programs?" she asked. "Everyone is so tired of grief."

I reminded her how important both topics had been since the pandemic. The grief retreat I'd established was especially sought after every year before the holidays.

Two people saying practically the same thing in one week? God often repeated his messages to me, validating the original one. I knew to pay attention. I wasn't at all surprised, then, when the woman who'd held my position before me came to my office on Friday morning.

"The programs you've brought here have been well received," she graciously opened the conversation, before hesitantly adding, "But I hate to tell you this. I'm hearing from others that they'd like less creativity and grief and more of what we used to have."

I calmly asked her what kind of programs she'd suggest. She visibly relaxed with my reaction.

"Oh, that's easy. Social justice. Or you could do something on Julian of Norwich."

I stifled back a chuckle. I didn't know who Julian of Norwich was, and didn't really care. God couldn't be more obvious, sending three different people in one week who basically said the same thing. Evidently, my creativity and grief programs were slated for the trash heap, and I'd be required to plan programs I wasn't the least bit interested in.

"I hope you don't resent me for telling you this," my predecessor said.

"It's just the opposite," I replied. "I feel like giving you a hug!" She hugged me before leaving, unaware her conversation had sealed the deal. I was going to resign.

I cried most of that weekend, dreading telling my boss on Monday. But by the time I turned in my thirty-day notice, I felt a deep sense of peace, confident in my decision. Even an offer of a raise and more flexible hours didn't tempt me to stay.

I didn't know what God had planned for me, but was certain it must be something amazing and significant. Maybe writing another book? Doing more public speaking? Nick was happy to drop most of his work hours. We talked about traveling together. Excited about our newly retired status, we were eager to see what God had in store for us.

Shortly after my resignation, Nick got a call from a long-time employee. Her husband was dying of cancer, and she wanted to spend time with him. We offered to take over her hours. For the next several weeks I worked at Nick's side, cleaning, serving lunches, and waitressing while he cooked, made drinks, and manned the register.

I remember one particularly busy day covering the lunch crowd. Exhausted by rushing from table to table taking orders, I perched on a stool to take a break. Leaning on the counter, I took a deep breath and looked around, studying my surroundings.

Really? I left my job for this? To clean and serve others, working for tips? I couldn't understand it. Why would God have me leave a good-paying job at a spirituality center to volunteer my time waitressing?

I couldn't understand it. Why would God have me leave a good-paying job at a spirituality center to volunteer my time waitressing?

My reverie was interrupted as a plate of food was placed in front of me. I turned to see the broad smile on my husband's face. Everything I needed to know was right there, reflected in his eyes. Gratitude. Companionship. Love. So much love.

God, in his infinite wisdom, had known exactly what He was doing when He led me to leave my job. He knew Nick would be called back to work and those weeks of working side by side would prepare us for what He had planned for us next as a couple.

Nick sold his business the following year. We moved to a Christian community, where we now co-coordinate an annual writer's conference. And that book and public speaking I thought God might have in store for me? Our God delights in surprises. Turns out, team Nick and Mary speak together on the power of prayer and co-wrote a book on the same topic.

Can't Claim Coincidence

Laura Bailey

. . . with all humility and gentleness, with patience, bearing with one another in love.

—Ephesians 4:2 (ESV)

I am grateful that my husband and I don't often argue, and when we do disagree, the arguments are resolved swiftly. However, not too long ago, we found ourselves in a pretty heated discussion that quickly morphed into a full-on marital spat. There was something I felt we needed to purchase for the home, and my husband couldn't justify the spending; no matter how hard we tried, we were at a standstill. While we have often gone to bed still upset, we've made up by the time we've had our first morning cup of coffee.

Not this time.

It was almost a week of coexisting; never had our house been so quiet! During that week of trading icy glares and the silent treatment, the Lord sent two friends to soften my heart and guide me to seek reconciliation with my husband, Tres, sooner rather than later.

Typically, when my husband and I engage in a marital spat, I vent to my gal pals in the hope of feeling vindicated or, at the very least, blowing off some steam. But not this time.

I remained tight-lipped, giving no indications of problems in paradise. If I'm honest, I didn't want to tell them because I knew I was in the wrong—but, pridefully and stubbornly, I wasn't ready to hear advice or even encouragement from well-meaning friends.

On the third day of our continued silent war, I received a call from a childhood friend. At the time I was on the way to dance practice with my three girls in the car, so I silenced the call and told myself I would call her back later. We typically got our families together in the summertime, and with the school year finishing soon, I assumed she was calling to

---

I replayed the message three more times, and each time I was amazed to hear the words that came out of the speaker.

---

make plans. Since we are both busy with work, families, and other responsibilities, we don't talk often, and it usually takes a massive game of phone tag and a few texts before we finally connect. So I was surprised when I saw a voicemail notification pop up a few minutes later.

After getting the girls settled into their classes, I listened to my friend's message outside. "Hey, I am not sure what's happening, but I needed to call you today. Is everything going OK with you and Tres? I felt the Lord leading me to pray for you all, so I did. But, well, I just hope everything is all right, and know either way, I am praying for your marriage. I am here if you need to talk."

I replayed the message three more times, and each time I was amazed to hear the words that came out of the speaker. I hadn't spoken to my friend in over a year. We were very close, but our conversations were typically hour-long catch-ups, trying to squeeze in a year's worth of information in an afternoon. We've talked about our marriages before, but since we both were in pretty spiritually grounded unions by God's grace, it didn't often come up.

My hand lingered over my friend's number, but I stared at the phone instead of calling her back.

My youngest daughter tapped me on the shoulder, breaking my daze. "Mom, it's time to go." On the ride home, I kept mentally replaying the message, finding it a coincidence that she would send it this week. For a brief moment, I pondered that perhaps the Lord was using my friend to nudge me to speak to my husband, but I didn't allow myself to linger on that thought. Instead, we arrived home, we ate dinner, and I went to bed sans conversing with my spouse.

A few more days passed, and my marriage was still at a standstill when I received a text from a friend at church.

"I am praying for you and Tres today," said the message that popped on the screen.

It wasn't odd for her to text me and share that she was praying for me; we were close and often randomly sent prayer requests and encouragement to each other. But this was the first time she mentioned my husband. I quickly responded with a "thank you." What had prompted her to send that message? I was grateful I would see her at church that night so I could find out.

When I asked her about it, she said she'd had a dream that my husband and I had gotten into a big fight and were considering separating. She said she woke up so upset; she'd never felt so worried about a dream before and immediately started praying for us and our marriage. She felt certain it was just a nightmare, but the Holy Spirit led her to reach out to me and pray on our behalf.

I immediately started crying. I shared with her the events of the last few days; while we'd never considered separating, we most certainly hadn't acted like two people who claim to love the Lord and each other. I confessed to her my unwillingness to be the first one to apologize and my childish, selfish behavior. I was sorry that the dream gave her such a fright, but I was so grateful that she acted on the prompting of the Holy Spirit to reach out to me. God was trying to get my attention and hold my heart through my two friends!

After my husband and I resolved our conflict that night, both apologizing for losing our tempers, we promised never to let our tempers and stubbornness get that out of control again. I always knew we would eventually work through it, but these women's actions led me to seek forgiveness sooner rather than later. The Lord used them and their willingness to be obedient to His leading to guide me to repentance and reconciliation in my marriage. I am so glad they listened and obeyed!

Lost Letters

Heather Jepsen

You make known to me the path of life; you will fill me with joy in your presence, with eternal pleasures at your right hand.

—PSALM 16:11 (NIV)

Have you ever had a moment where nothing seemed to be going your way? I sure did! I was in my early twenties when I felt the call from God to be a pastor. I was a music major at the time, studying the harp, but I felt such a tugging in my heart to change direction that I had to follow to see where it would lead.

I spent my senior year of college visiting seminaries and making plans to attend one so I could begin the path to ordained ministry. After visiting a famous, very old seminary on the East Coast, I felt certain that God was calling me to go there for my learning. I was so certain that it was the only school I applied to.

I got busy that spring filling out all my application materials and soliciting all the letters of recommendation that I would need. I asked some of my favorite professors in the music department to write letters for me. It wasn't a big ask;

I had won the senior award for outstanding academics and musicianship that year, after all. I was the top student in my graduation class, so a letter of recommendation should have been easy.

As spring dragged on, I began to wonder why I had not heard from the seminary about my acceptance. I phoned their registration office and discovered that they were missing one of my recommendation letters. *That's weird*, I thought.

I went to Professor Anna, the person whose letter was missing, and asked her about it. "I sent that letter months ago," she said. "Don't know why they didn't get it, but I will send it again."

I could not understand why God would call me
to ministry and then slam the door in my face.

Weeks went by, and still no word. Again, I phoned the seminary, and again they said that I was missing that letter of recommendation. *What in the world?* I thought.

Again, I went to Professor Anna. I was so embarrassed to have to ask again and to imply that she hadn't done the thing I had requested and that she clearly said she had done. She was upset.

"Look," she said, "I wrote that letter and sent it twice. I will try again, but I don't know what you expect me to do. Sounds like the problem is on their end."

Time passed, and the window to choose and attend schools began to close. When I still hadn't heard from the seminary,

I called the registration office a third time. "Still no letter," was the reply. *I can't believe this!* I thought.

I was torn. Was that teacher lying to me? Did she not want me to switch careers, and that was why she was blocking my path to seminary? I couldn't believe that sweet professor Anna would do such a thing. But I wasn't about to ask her again.

I decided to approach another teacher, Professor Dan.

"Dan," I said, "I'm kind of in a bind. Would you be able to write a letter of recommendation for me? It's already past due, but I can't seem to get one from Professor Anna."

"Sure," he said. "Happy to help."

I waited and prayed. *Maybe this time things will work.* Weeks passed and still no word. When I finally called the seminary, I felt like I knew the answer before I heard it. They still had no letter of recommendation for me. I hung up the phone in tears.

I had only applied to one school, and at this point it was too late to apply anywhere else. I was about to graduate, and I had no plans, no future, nothing. I could not understand why God would call me to ministry and then slam the door in my face.

I did the only thing I knew how to do; I turned to God in prayer. "God, I only seek to follow Your call. Help me to see the path. I am lost."

Over time I began to wonder if perhaps God was closing this door on purpose. Maybe those letters weren't really lost after all. Maybe God was telling me that this wasn't the right time for seminary. Or maybe God was telling me that this particular school wasn't the right place for me. I began to open myself to the possibility of not going to the seminary that fall and remaining where I was for another year. As I began to mull that idea over, I felt settled and certain. I knew I was right. God didn't want that path for me. I needed to wait until another path made itself plain.

Then, out of the blue, I got a call from the seminary. "We have decided to admit you for study," said the person on the other end of the line. "As long as you get that last letter to us, you can begin training in the fall."

I took a deep breath. *This is so crazy. I can't believe I'm about to do this,* I thought, but I held my ground. "No" I replied. "I don't think that is the plan God has for me right now. Thank you anyway."

It was a hard decision, for sure. I had to explain to my parents that I had changed my mind, that I wouldn't go to seminary that fall after all. They were so worried that I had abandoned the plan altogether.

I had to get a job to make some money and keep myself busy for a year, and then I had to start applying to schools all over again.

But it turned out to be a good year for me. I worked as a waitress. I took on some leadership roles in my local church. I even took some extra classes at the university I had graduated from. And when the time came, I applied to more than one seminary. Still, I worried that maybe I wasn't supposed to be a pastor after all. In the back of my mind, I began to doubt God's call.

When the time came to choose, this time around I was much more grounded and focused on listening for God's direction. I visited a school on the West Coast, the farthest away I could have gotten from the one I almost went to the year before, and while there I looked and listened like I never had before.

As I worshipped in the chapel, the sun came shining through the stained glass and lit up the pew around me. I felt anointed and I began to cry. *This is the right choice,* I thought. *Thank You, God, for making Your will clear to me.*

I returned home and, as I am sure you can guess, was immediately informed I had been accepted to the West Coast school. That coming fall, I moved to California, and within a few weeks I met the man who would be my husband. Of course, I didn't know that at the time! He was just another student beginning school at the same time as me, but he was one of the many surprises God had in store for me.

It's been more than twenty-five years now since those lost letters. I never did figure out what happened, though sometimes I still wonder about the possibilities. All I'm sure about is that it was too much of a coincidence to not be the hand of God.

I sometimes wonder what would have happened if I went to that other school. I am glad I didn't. I learned such important lessons in that year, and I have lived my life differently ever since. I no longer make my own plans and forge ahead. Instead, I pray, I listen, and I follow my God.

I look around now at my husband, my children, and the wonderful church I serve, and I know that none of this would have been possible if I hadn't looked for God's message in a perplexing series of events. We often say that when God closes a door, He opens a window. Now I say that when a letter gets lost—listen.

God's Mysterious Ways: When God Repeats Himself

We can all be hard of hearing sometimes. Jesus was fond of saying, "He who has ears, let him hear." God is so patient with us. He doesn't put His hands on His hips and look at us sternly saying, "I've told you this over and over again." In His infinite kindness, He just keeps saying what He needs us to hear over and over again until we finally get it.

What's the best way to listen for God's repetition?

- **Pray.** The prayer "Help me to see what I'm not seeing" can help us remember to keep our eyes and ears open to God's voice. As the stories from our writers remind us, God will keep trying to send us the message we need.

- **Seek.** It's much easier to hear God's voice when whatever vies for our attention is quieted. Where can you find silence in your day? Does first thing in the morning work for you? Or maybe late at night when everyone else in your household is asleep. Maybe taking a midday walk with soft instrumental music playing through headphones can help center your attention.

- **Act.** Try taking some time each day, whenever works best for you, to be still and quiet. Ask God to help you see what you've been missing from Him.

- **Reflect.** How does the idea of just sitting and being quiet with God feel to you? If the quiet isn't working for you, what other times and places might you find to be open to God's leading?

A Light in the Night

Raylene Nickel

For I know the plans I have for you, says the LORD,
plans for welfare and not for evil, to give
you a future and a hope.

—JEREMIAH 29:11 (RSV)

I don't see how I can do it; it feels impossible," I told my friends Kathy and Bev as we walked across one of the paddocks on my farm in North Dakota. "I'd have to borrow the money to buy the rest of this farm, and it just seems like too big a loan for me to repay all by myself."

My friends looked at me compassionately but said nothing. What could they say? They knew little about my finances or the dreams I'd shared with my husband, John, who had died the summer before. They'd traveled from Manitoba just to see how I was doing. I hadn't seen them for a year, and we rarely spoke by phone or email.

The three of us walked in silence for a while. After a few minutes, I said, "C'mon, I'll show you my cows."

We found the herd grazing contentedly at the end of one of the paddocks. This particular paddock happened to have some weeds in it. "After the cows are finished grazing the grass, I'll hire a neighbor to cut the weeds down with his tractor and sickle mower," I said.

That was something John would have thought of doing, too. Together, we always thought of ways to make our farm better. We tried to make the pastures more productive, the soil richer, the cattle healthier and happier. We loved our work. In fact, work bordered on recreation.

There was just one niggling frustration—or maybe it was more of a sadness. We were investing all of our tender loving care into a farm still partly owned by other people who were not involved in the day-to-day work. John and I had dreamed and dreamed, and prayed and prayed, to own the family farm fully ourselves. Not for profit or gain, but to simply have complete freedom to care for the farm in ways unique to us. And in the end, after we were older and through working, we hoped to have the complete freedom to gift it to a younger, deserving farmer of our choosing.

This was all hard to explain to my friends. After they returned home, I was left alone with my thoughts. And alone with the work. I was sixty-one, and the daily work was often challenging and all-consuming. True, because of downsizing, my herd was smaller than it had been when John and I worked together, but my work was solitary now. I fixed fences, pumped water for cattle, and moved them from pasture to pasture by myself. Young neighbors harvested the hay from the hayfields, and we each took a share of the hay crop. With my own equipment I hauled my share of the bales in from the fields to stock the winter feeding areas. All the while I continued my work as a freelance agricultural journalist.

I had plenty of time to think as I worked. And remember. Twenty-five years earlier, John had sold his small farm in Manitoba to move with me to this larger farm, which was then owned by my mother. This farm offered more room for growth, and just as John had owned his farm in Manitoba, we dreamed of owning this farm also. We hoped to buy it over time from my mother, and she had tentatively agreed to the sale.

But in time she changed her mind, and upon her death the farm passed into the hands of her four children, including me. John and I ended up being partners with people who didn't want to be involved in running the farm.

The years passed, and family dynamics combined with financial and weather setbacks caused John and me to be more and more discouraged about ever really owning the farm. But although our ownership prospects looked bleak, we threw ourselves increasingly into building the health of the farm's soils, forages, and cattle.

Privately, however, I never lost hope of one day fully owning our farm. It seemed unjust to me that John should have sacrificed his own small farm in Manitoba to move to a farm he might not ever own. It also seemed unjust that we, as the people doing the work, should not wholly own the property. At one point, my internal struggle became so great that I began a forty-day prayer crusade devoted to examining our motives for desiring to own the farm. I prayed for the understanding of what my actions might have on my extended family. I prayed for special blessings upon each family member from whom I hoped we might one day buy their share of the farm.

In 2010, twenty-one years after we had moved to the farm, we got a loan to buy my late oldest brother's share from his daughters. Three years later, John's long illness worsened, and we sold two-thirds of the cow herd to lighten our workload. The money went to pay for part of my older sister's share.

Then John died. I sold more cows to finish paying off my sister and kept up with payments on the earlier land note and other farm loans for machinery and farm infrastructure improvements.

At the time of my Manitoba friends' visit, I was still reeling from grief over John's death and often bowled over by the labor and business demands of the farm. Still, comfort came from my memories of John's deep love for his farm and how he had cared for it as if it were his own personal child. Only months before his death, he had stood at the living room window gazing out upon the land. "I love our place; I love what we do here," he said.

Privately, however, I never lost hope of one day fully owning our farm.

But without John, our dream of physically owning the farm now seemed impossible. Borrowing the money to buy the last farm share from my second-older brother seemed risky. I still had some farm loans to pay, and my income was diminished because of the downsizing of the cow herd. My freelance writing did provide other income, but that was always uncertain. I was simply afraid to take out a loan from the bank.

It seemed that God heard my fears. One night, not long after my friends' visit, I was awakened from sleep by a brilliant light.

Through my bedroom windows I could see the light flooding the backyard and illuminating my bed. I smiled sleepily, thinking the lovely light came from a full moon. But the next morning, as I was recording daily weather events in my calendar, I discovered that the moon that night had been a new moon, a dark moon.

I was flooded with awe. What had it been? There was no outdoor light that could have accounted for what I saw—it was always dark outside my house at night. And my house was a quarter-mile from the nearest road, too far for the light to have come from a passing vehicle. There was only one explanation: God had sent the light.

Starting that day, a new courage began to flow into me, and my fear about finances began to ebb. I began to believe that if I borrowed the money to pay for my brother's share of the farm, God would watch over me to ensure that I could pay it back. Even so, it was several weeks before I pulled together the confidence to go and fill out the application. I was still apprehensive as I filled out the paperwork, but my lender's approval came so easily that I felt God's hand over the entire process.

It took eight years to pay off that loan, but I am now debt free and own the farm fully. After so many years of hard work and hope, that feels like a miracle to me. That night God sent His light, He showed me that what I dream, He will in His time empower me to do.

God's Retirement Plan

Jack Stagge, as told to Stephanie Thompson

*Behold, I will do a new thing, now it shall spring forth;
shall you not know it? I will even make a road in the
wilderness and rivers in the desert.*

—ISAIAH 43:19 (NKJV)

My accountant pushed away from his computer and extended his hand. "Congratulations, Jack! Keep working and saving. In seven more years, you'll have a comfortable retirement."

I shook his hand, thanked him, and walked to my truck. *If I keep working, I can retire at sixty-two and be set. If I quit now, I wouldn't have enough to make it through my retirement years.* It was a clear-cut decision, but I felt torn. Ever since my wife, Holly, and I had gone on a mission trip to Tanzania last year, I'd yearned to go back—not just for a week or two, but for months at a time to really make a difference.

Until now, my life had unfolded just as I'd planned. At sixteen, I decided to go into the medical profession. A good student, I excelled at math and science, but that wasn't the primary reason I chose a health care career. Growing up, my parents gave my sister and me lots of love, but money was scarce. My parents both worked to make ends meet.

Materially, things were lean, but spiritually we were fed by my parent's strong faith—bedtime and mealtime prayers, memorizing scriptures, worshipping together at church. Still, I wanted more financial security as an adult. My plan was to have a high-paying job and a hefty income once I was grown.

At San Diego State University, I majored in anatomy. I met Holly my senior year. Petite, tanned, with long brown hair, we talked the entire evening on the beach the night we met. Also interested in healthcare, she was an audiology major. We married eighteen months later.

From San Diego we moved to Fresno. I earned a physical therapy degree and did postgraduate work at the University of Southern California. After completing my residency, I found a couple of partners and opened an orthopedics and sports rehabilitation center. Business boomed. Within three years, my school and company loans were paid off. My family was on track, too. We had a spacious house on a hill with a swimming pool in the backyard. Holly stayed home and cared for our three children, Sarah, Heidi, and Justin, all about two years apart.

In contrast to my own childhood, my family had everything they wanted. We never had to do without because something was too expensive. Still, we didn't want our kids to grow up spoiled. We were involved in church—Sunday mornings, Sunday nights, Wednesday evenings. Holly and I became youth sponsors when the kids got to be teens. We took several mission trips to Mexico, telling people about Jesus and holding vacation Bible school. It was fun and rewarding.

Now our kids were grown and living on their own. Holly and I loved traveling and planned to do more once I retired.

The logical decision was to keep working, keep saving, and in seven years my retirement income would fund our adventures. I didn't mind serving God full-time once I retired. In fact, that was my plan.

Then, some adults at church wanted to take a mission trip to Africa. We'd never been there, so Holly googled "mission trips to Africa." Websites popped up. She emailed them all, asking for information on two-week mission opportunities.

"I had an urgent reply from a missionary in Arusha, Tanzania," said Holly the next night at the dinner table. "He said: We are in desperate need of help. Please come."

"Some Maasai people have walked two days for the medicine you're bringing," the missionary explained.

"Did you tell him we could do a medical clinic, construction, and Bible programs?"

She nodded. "Anything we wanted to do was fine. He was very eager."

While we waited for packets from several other organizations that week, the Arusha missionary emailed again. "When are you coming? We need you."

Other organizations had specific needs and requirements, but in Arusha they made volunteering easy. They didn't care what we did, as long as we came.

Nine months later, Holly and I left with five church friends. After several layovers on our thirty-hour trip to Nairobi,

Kenya, we piled into a van for the five-hour drive to Arusha. At the Arusha missionary base, a security guard met us in front of the ten-foot fence that surrounded a compound of simple, concrete buildings.

"Looks more like a prison than a mission," I whispered to Holly, who stared wide-eyed. We took our suitcases to our modest room, crawled under the mosquito net, and sank into bed.

At dawn, we began the two-hour drive through the bush to the village of Engikaret, which means "a place of dust." There was no pavement or roads; we were just four-wheeling over the parched ground. When we arrived, we discovered that life at the village centered around cattle, goat, and sheep herding. *Bomas*—stick-framed huts covered with a mixture of mud and dung—were surrounded by a fence made from acacia thorns and branches. "Keeps lions and hyenas out," confided the missionary as he pointed to the fence.

The arid, barren landscape paled in comparison to the Maasai's dark skin and colorful traditional robes. Yet their manner was as dry as the desert. Eyes downcast, they turned away when we spoke.

A long line of waiting people snaked around the *bomas*. "Some Maasai people have walked two days for the medicine you're bringing," the missionary explained.

We set up the medical clinic inside a building with no running water, no electricity, and a squatty potty outside. All we had was a nurse, myself, and non-medical volunteers with a few boxes of supplies. I knew right away it wouldn't be enough.

The medical needs ranged from diseases such as typhoid, tuberculosis, and AIDS to infected wounds that leaked pus and broken bones that hadn't been properly set. Antibiotics were only a Band-Aid for these ailments. We treated 385 locals that day and had to turn some people away after dark. They were all dehydrated. Some admitted to not having a drink for days, since the nearest water source was nineteen miles away.

The two weeks flew by, filled with medical trips to neighboring villages, building constructions, and Bible programs with the children. Our team was overwhelmed by the need but energized to be used by God.

"There's so much more we could do," I told Holly as we packed to leave. "The drinking water's not safe. One in four Maasai die before age four."

At that moment, I heard an audible voice. You're home.

If we really wanted to make a difference, we'd need to stay for months at a time to assess needs and build relationships. Our hearts went out to these people. How could we not want to help them?

We told the missionary so, but he cautioned us, "Don't make a quick decision. Go home. Pray and think about it for eighteen months." He wanted us to make sure it was a calling from God and not an emotional decision.

So that's where we were at the time of my accountant visit. Holly and I prayed about spending more time in Tanzania, but there were so many obstacles. My partners and patients depended on me. Two weeks off a couple of times a year was all I could do so I didn't stress out my partners, who handled my workload when I was gone.

Besides, what if Holly or I got sick or disabled? How would I provide without a nest egg? Our kids were in their twenties and our first grandchild was born weeks ago. Yes, working the next seven years until retirement age was the sensible thing to do. My accountant had agreed with my plan to provide a comfortable life for my family.

As I drove home, I pushed the conflict out of my mind. It had been less than a year since our initial visit. Now a dozen of us would be making a return trip to the Arusha base in a few weeks. We'd be better prepared and equipped this time. *Lord, I want to help out, but You know my plan. This is our home.*

Back in Engikaret, my heartbeat quickened. The women, who spoke through an interpreter, marveled that we'd come back. Shy gazes looked away when our eyes met, but they didn't turn completely away like our first visit.

Again, we held a medical clinic, and at the same time worked on constructing a better-equipped building to treat patients and staff housing. We'd brought a corn grinder for the village women to use to make food preparations simpler. They were astonished, not only by how quickly it ground the corn, but more so because we gave it to them. It was the only item they'd ever owned. Our two weeks there flew by once again. The next morning, we planned to head home.

Birds stirred outside as the first rays of dawn peeked above the horizon. Hens clucked, roosters crowed, and dogs barked to signal the beginning of our last day. I slowly roused awake.

In that place between awakening and sleeping, I lay— half-praying, half-dreaming, trying to keep still so I wouldn't disturb Holly. The familiar tug-of-war had already started in my heart: The Maasai people here, or my comfortable, predictable life at home.

As usual, the possibilities flooded my mind. My money, my practice, or an unsecure future. Could we make it back home if we got sick or were just plain tired of the overwhelming, never-ending need? *God, I don't understand. If this is where You want me to be and if the time is now, You have to make it clear.*

At that moment, I heard an audible voice. *You're home.*

Stunned and shocked, I leaned up on one elbow and strained my ear to hear through the sounds of the bush waking up. But as quickly as it came, the voice was gone. I rolled over.

"Did you hear that?" I asked Holly.

"Hmmm?" she answered sleepily.

I figured it must have been a dog bark or animal shriek. It just *sounded* like someone said those words: *you're home.* After all, I was half-asleep.

I rubbed Holly's arm affectionately. "How are you feeling?"

She looked at me with her shiny brown eyes, her lips parted softly in a smile. "I feel like we're home."

Holy chills ran down my back. God's message was clear. This wasn't an emotional decision, and we didn't need to wait any longer. Relief swept over me. We were called. We had a new home and a new plan.

That summer, I sold my physical therapy practice, and we put our house on the market. Some people thought we were crazy, but I didn't care.

Eighteen years later, Holly and I now spend half the year working with the Maasai people, educating the women and teaching them trades, schooling the children, and helping the people get their basic needs met with clean water sources.

The other half of the year, I fill in for vacationing physical therapists, lecture at colleges, and raise money for the non-profit agency we started called Faces for Hope. We've built a medical clinic, a school, and a safe house for orphans and girls at risk of becoming child brides. We ensure that the village has a clean water source and provide medical supplies. We've even helped start a church in a remote part of Maasailand.

My life hasn't turned out exactly like I planned. Each year, I leave the comforts of America and go live in the thorns and dust of Tanzania. Hot showers are exchanged for a cloth and a bucket of cold water. Restaurant meals are replaced by corn mash patties, rice, or beans. The Maasai women who were so shy at first now meet our gaze, smile, and laugh with us.

I don't worry about retirement, the "what if's," or having an affluent lifestyle anymore. The same sovereign God who sent me to bring His hope to the Maasai people manages my retirement plan. God has made a home for us in two places. I don't know what the future holds, but I know the One who holds the future. To know I am right where God wants me is a place of comfort, a true home. My plan was a comfortable life for my family, but God's plan is even better.

The Traveling Matches

Nancy Schrock

Surely the righteous will never be shaken;
they will be remembered forever.

—PSALM 112:6 (NIV)

In 2019, I moved from Florida to Albuquerque, New Mexico. I posted the move on Facebook, and one of my high-school classmates from Marion, Illinois, contacted me to say that she lived in Albuquerque too, and she suggested that we should get together. We hadn't known each other in high school, but after having lunch together a few times, we became good friends. Susan had lived in the area for decades, so she was full of good advice on what to see and where to go. And as we got to know each other, she told me things about herself that I had never known—for example, that in the 1970s her dad had run a small oil company called Etherton Oil. At the time, it was just a fun fact about her past, but it would become an opportunity for us both to see God at work in our lives.

In 2020, my older son finished up his graduate work at Ohio State, landed a job in Albuquerque, and moved his family out to New Mexico. One day, I was over at his house, where he was still in the process of unpacking the boxes from the move. Among my son's own things were some items that my father—who was in his nineties and not in good health—had passed on to my son when he was cleaning out his house. My son pointed to one box and said, "That has some of Grandpa's old hunting jackets in it. I'm not going to keep them. Would you want them?"

I hated to dispose of anything of my dad's without taking a careful look at it, so I took the box home with me. I clearly remember taking the box over to the garbage can and pulling out one of the jackets. It was dirty and stained—not anything I would keep or even give away. But before throwing it away, I decided to go through the pockets. Maybe he had put something in there of sentimental value.

The jacket pockets held two shotgun shells and an old book of matches. Not the keepsakes I was hoping for, but not safe to just throw in the garbage, either. I set the shells aside and examined the matchbook. It looked old enough that the matches might not light anymore. Then I noticed what was written on the cover: *Etherton Oil Co., Complete Auto and Industrial Lubricants, N. Fair Street, Marion, Illinois.*

I was stunned. How could this be? The matches were from Susan's father's business!

I called Susan. "You'll never guess what I found," I told her, texting her a photo of the matchbook.

"Oh, my." I could hear the excitement in her voice. "I don't have one of these. I have an old Etherton Oil pen, but no matches." After a thoughtful pause, she added, "They must be old. My father sold the business in 1978, and it changed names when it changed owners. There's not much left from that time."

"Well, then you should have it."

This was during the Covid lockdown, when we couldn't come to each other's houses, so we met at a local park and I gave her the matches. Joy radiated from her face. "I can't believe you found this," she said as she held her new treasure. "This is a true God moment."

"It surely is," I told her. "Funny how I was looking for a keepsake from my father and found one from yours."

What are the odds of this happening? As we spoke, we reconstructed the chain of events that had to have occurred for the matches to end up with her. Sometime in the 1970s, my father must have gone into Etherton Oil in Marion,

---

Joy radiated from her face. "I can't believe you found this," she said as she held her new treasure. "This is a true God moment."

Illinois. That wouldn't have been unusual; the shop was only a few blocks from where we lived. While he was in there, he picked up a book of matches. They were one of the free giveaways, along with pens. We could tell from examining the book that my father used a couple of the matches, probably to start a fire to burn leaves or trash. Perhaps it was in the autumn, because he then put them in the pocket of his hunting jacket along with a couple of shotgun shells. (Dad was a good man, but not big on safety.)

The matches stayed in that jacket, along with the shotgun shells, for over forty years, until my father was cleaning out some old belongings and gave the box of jackets to my older son. My son took the box to Columbus, Ohio, and put it in storage without ever opening it. The movers certainly didn't investigate the box, or they would never have moved ammunition and matches to Albuquerque. That box of jackets—ones that my son didn't even want but for some reason kept—made their way clear across the country, waiting for the day when my son happened to ask me if I wanted the box. I took it home and made the effort to go through the pockets. If any one of those things hadn't happened, I never would have found that keepsake for Susan, a high-school classmate whom I had just become friends with a few months before—and the only classmate living in Albuquerque, so far from where we grew up.

Those matches traveled 1,100 miles and waited more than forty years to touch the life of a loving daughter—a special God moment that I was privileged to witness.

The Move

Jeanette Levellie

—⟨✿⟩—

*"And I will provide a place for my people Israel
and will plant them so that they can have a
home of their own and no longer be disturbed."*

—2 SAMUEL 7:10 (NIV)

My husband, Kevin, and I loved pastoring. At least one of us did. Before I married Kevin in 1975, he'd pastored his first church in Fresno, California, for a year. I fell in love with the *idea* of becoming a pastor's wife. My imagination was full of exciting and romantic scenes: Serving God's people who needed to grow in the Lord. Teaching little ones about Jesus. Encouraging Kevin when he was down. What a grand adventure waited!

A few weeks after our honeymoon, I discovered the realities of helping my man lead a congregation. I wasn't mature enough in my faith to help anything grow besides the camellia bush beside our front porch. My idea of service was singing in the choir and a lot of smiling. I liked the three- and four-year-olds in my Sunday school class, but I liked sleeping in more. Kevin had to call my substitute teacher half the time. And it never occurred to me that to encourage Kevin, he'd have to be discouraged. I ranted about how immature people acted when they complained about his lawn cutting skills or the color of the kitchen. But—surprise, surprise—my getting angry on his behalf didn't make Kev feel better.

I loved my husband. But I didn't love the life I'd chosen.

After fifteen years of pastoring five California churches, Kevin lost his pastorate due to lack of funding for his position. Every new door of ministry Kevin knocked on slammed in his face. Desperate for a paycheck to provide for us and our two children, he took a job in a downtown L.A. collection agency. Kev started out as a helper to the vice president, a position he jokingly called "a gopher." When other workers left, the company's owner gave Kevin their jobs. Within a few years, Kev managed the entire office singlehandedly. His boss was generous, giving Kevin a raise every year. And Kev enjoyed the work, which consisted mostly of accounting and data entry. But he was miserable. In moments when we were alone he often said, "I'm praying that God will teach me contentment. But I really miss preaching and teaching God's Word."

I, on the other hand, was elated. I could now attend church each Sunday and worship with no worries that people would scrutinize the clothes I wore or how I raised my kids. No one expected me to rush next door to the parsonage and change the empty toilet paper rolls in the ladies room. No one asked me why my husband didn't trim his beard as closely as they thought he should. I felt like I could finally live as an ordinary human being.

⁂

While Kev worked in the business world, he continued to send out résumés. Churches in Ohio, Missouri, Delaware, and West

Virginia asked Kevin to interview and preach a trial sermon. With each congregation, a crazy circumstance kept us in L.A. One rejected us because we homeschooled our kids. Another didn't like the idea that I was Charismatic. A church in West Virginia wanted to hire Kevin. But when we couldn't sell our home after six months of trying, Kev had to call and tell them to look elsewhere.

I prayed with my husband for God to open the right ministry door. Looking back, I doubt my heart agreed with my mouth. I was happier than I'd been in over two decades. I loved my job managing the music department of a huge

---

I prayed with my husband for God to open the right ministry door. Looking back, I doubt my heart agreed with my mouth.

Christian bookstore. I loved my friends and prayer partners. I loved the Southern California weather and all the excellent restaurants (eating out is my favorite sport).

While eating chocolate cake and chatting with friends at my birthday party in 1999, our phone rang. I could tell by Kevin's happy tone of voice that it was a church calling. He'd been out of the pulpit for ten years, and he was desperate to return to preaching. Kev put his hand over the receiver and whispered, "A congregation in Paris, Illinois, wants us to fly there for a week to try out. What do you say?"

I blurted, "I don't want to go to *Illinois!*" Nevertheless, I reluctantly agreed to travel with Kev, just to make him happy.

When I saw the look of relief and hope in his eyes, my heart softened. A little.

Kevin and the lead elder, Jim, scheduled our visit for Labor Day weekend, two weeks later. Although I'd agreed to fly across the country to support my husband, I still had a wall of reluctance around my heart for all we'd endured in previous churches. I didn't want to get back into church leadership and open myself to further pain.

Everything changed on a bright Saturday morning a few days after my birthday. I stood near the bay window in our dining room, folding clothes on the dining table. When the phone rang, I put down a towel to answer it.

"May I please speak with Kevin?" a kind, friendly man said.

I explained that Kev was out and asked if I could take a message.

"This is Jim from the Nevins church in Paris, Illinois." Of course I recognized the name, and we began to chat. I expected that it would be only a few minutes of casual conversation, but suddenly a bit of chit-chat about the climate in southern Illinois versus southern California turned to deeper subjects of careers, marriage, and ministry. Jim's wife was going through some major health issues. As he described her anguish, the warmth in Jim's voice and his concern for his wife softened my heart a little more.

I felt God nudge me to pray for them—right then, out loud. Praying with strangers over the phone wasn't something I did often. I rarely prayed aloud with anyone but my family and very close friends. But the urge to pray with Jim propelled me forward. "May I pray for you and your congregation?" I asked. Jim was all for it. As if God had prepared both our hearts for this holy moment.

When he gave his assent, words began to pour out of me. "Father, we need your wisdom and guidance. You have always treated us so well, out of your heart of love. Please show Jim how to best help his wife, and how to best proceed in their congregation's search for a pastor." As I talked to God, the walls of anger around my heart began to crumble and dissolve. I felt the warmth of the Holy Spirit's embrace envelope me. God was giving me a late birthday gift, not just a sweet moment to treasure, but the key to our family's future. I said goodbye to Jim—who had been quiet throughout the entire prayer—so I could savor the feeling of Jesus's presence.

I looked up and said with a choked voice, "Lord, if I'm the one who's holding Kevin back from his dream, I surrender."

Afterward I stood in my dining room, the August sun warming my face from the window. I looked up and said with a choked voice, "Lord, if I'm the one who's holding Kevin back from his dream, I surrender. You know I love being a 'nobody.' You know how happy I am in our life here. But I don't want to stand in Your way if You want Kev back in the ministry." I took a deep breath, knelt on the rug and with a shaky voice said, "Not my will, but Yours be done."

When Kev came home, I didn't share with him right away that wonder-filled, intimate moment with God. While I helped him unload apples, cheeses, and coffee, I was quiet. I wanted to savor the miraculous change of heart I'd experienced and hold it deep within. The memory seemed too holy to share with anyone, even my husband.

A couple weeks later, when the wheels of our jet touched down on the runway, an explosion of joy went off in my chest. We hadn't even met any of the people in Paris. Kevin hadn't preached his trial sermon or met with the elders. But I knew. This was home.

For the first time in almost twenty-five years, I was excited at the thought of being a pastor's wife.

Soon we discovered why the Lord chose Paris, Illinois, as our new home. One generous church member took us shopping for new all-season wardrobes and new furniture. Others invited us to share holiday meals in their home; some treated us to meals out. A deacon who loved to garden spent hours planting veggies and coached us how to tend them. The Sunday we shared our bounty of green beans, lovely red tomatoes, and sweet peppers, he stood next to us as people filed out of church and said, "I taught them everything they know." Laughter filled the vestibule.

The community also welcomed Kevin and me. The editor of the local paper gave me the opportunity to write an inspirational column every week, leading to several book contracts. And more than one neighbor offered us free kittens.

One icy morning as Kevin drove me to work, we slid into a ditch. We quickly skidded back out and were on our way again—unknowingly leaving his back bumper behind. A neighbor recognized our car and retrieved the bumper. When Kevin returned home, the twisted bumper sat on our front porch.

Looking back twenty-five years later, we've waded though some messes. A few that caused Kev and I to look at each other and say, "Did you ever think...?" But we've experienced more miracles than messes. Astonishing healings. People giving their lives to Jesus. And a church family that loves *and likes* each other.

Hundreds of times I've walked with Kevin across the gravel from our church to the parsonage and said, "I love living here!" God knew we needed these warm, caring Midwesterners to nourish our souls with His unconditional love. To heal us from the past. To help me believe that ministry can be joyful and fulfilling.

If I hadn't been the one to pick up the call from Jim that morning... would we have missed an opportunity that turned out to be perfect for our entire family?

I merely had to yield my heart to God. To surrender my will to His, and let Him change my mind. If I hadn't been the one to pick up the call from Jim that morning, if I hadn't felt moved to pray for him, would I have come to the trial preaching with a hard heart, not wanting to leave our California home? Would we have missed an opportunity that turned out to be perfect for our entire family?

Two Sundays ago, our congregation honored Kevin for his faithful twenty-five years of service. When Jim stood at the end of the worship service he said, "Twenty-five years ago when I looked at Kevin's résumé I said, "This guy is super overqualified for our little country church. And then we met Kevin and Jeanette. They were warm, down-to-earth, but serious about walking with Jesus. So we hired them. But shortly after they moved here and I heard Kevin's remarkable preaching, I told my wife, 'They'll never stay.'" The laughter echoed around the entire sanctuary. And then Jim turned to us, his voice breaking a bit as he said, "I'm glad I was wrong."

My House

Judy Spence, as told to Stephanie Thompson

Trust in the LORD with all your heart, and lean not on your own understanding; in all your ways submit to him, and he will make your paths straight.

—PROVERBS 3:5–6 (NIV)

I slumped in the chair at my computer desk as I scrolled through the listings on the link my real estate agent had emailed. So far, I'd seen nowhere I wanted to live. After having the same house for three decades, my husband and I had decided to sell our place and find something new. I yearned for a home I could be excited about, a newer construction with the features and amenities I'd dreamed of— gated community, a small lawn, three-car garage, spacious kitchen, and extra bedrooms and bathrooms to accommodate my out-of-town daughter and her family when they visited. I'd looked at a lot of properties and as far as I could see, the house of my dreams—a house that felt as if it was truly made for me—didn't exist. Or at least, it wasn't for sale right now.

Discouraged, I clicked out of the Multiple Listing Service (MLS) real estate database. Maybe it was better that I couldn't seem to find the perfect house, because the sale of my own home had mysteriously stalled. The whole process was unnerving. I couldn't afford to buy a new house until my current one sold. But what if mine was sold and I couldn't find a place I'd rather live? Or what if I found the perfect house and didn't have a buyer for mine? It was an intricate process that only added to my worry and stress.

My current house had languished on the market for a couple months. Weeks ago, Larry, a friend from church who was also my real estate agent, called. "A buyer's interested. She plans to make an offer in a few days."

How could this be my house when someone else was set to buy it? How could the house God had pointed out to me already be sold?

But after a week, we'd heard nothing. Larry checked back a few times, hosted an open house and had a few showings, but no new parties were interested and the one buyer who said she was sending an offer never did.

That Sunday when I saw Larry at church, I suggested he take my house off the market. "Winter's coming. Maybe it's not the right time," I said.

Larry shook his head. "You've got to trust God, Judy. It's only been a couple months."

Six weeks from when that buyer first expressed interest, her agent finally sent a contract. Larry called with the good news. I was ecstatic!

"She wants to close in a month," said Larry. "I'll email you the current MLS link. It's time to find your new house!"

As I hung up the telephone, joy was replaced by a flood of panic. *What if I can't find the perfect house?* Back at my computer, I opened the link and pored over all the available homes in my price range, sixty-three listings in all. *Not the best location. No curb appeal. The bedrooms are too small.* There was something I didn't like about each of them. The more homes I looked at, the more discouraged I became. A few were OK, but I couldn't envision living in any of them.

Then I clicked on the listing for a house on Jefferson Lane. It was amazing! A builder's show home with many upgrades, including stained, stamped concrete on the front walk, a decorative tile design in the foyer, custom bay windows, and wood blinds. Additionally, it was in a gated community where most of the residents were retirees like me. Small yards that were cared for by the homeowners' association. A three-car garage, spacious kitchen with a generous island, and two spare bedrooms with a Jack-and-Jill bathroom in between for guests. Built just six years ago. I loved it. It was everything I'd hoped for in a home and more—the perfect house. As I stared at my computer monitor, a strange knowing came over me. A divine thought entered my mind: this was my house.

I called Larry and gave him the MLS number. He looked it up. Moments later, he called me back.

"I'm sorry, Judy," he said. "That Jefferson Lane property has been under contract for six weeks. I just talked to the Realtor. The inspections are done, and she's certain the sale will go through; in fact, they're closing tomorrow."

Larry kept talking, but I'd quit listening. How could this be my house when someone else was set to buy it? How could the house God had pointed out to me already be sold?

We hung up. I walked to the living room and plopped in a chair. *Now what, Lord?* I'd never heard God whisper so strongly. *Was I wrong?* Larry had encouraged me to look at the listings again and email him with a few we could tour tomorrow. I did.

That night I couldn't sleep. I kept thinking about that house on Jefferson Lane. *My house.* An idea floated through my mind: Tell Larry to talk to the Realtor again. Let him know he has a client who is ready to buy that house immediately. *They've done the inspection. They're ready to close,* I argued with myself. But somehow, I couldn't let go of the idea that this was the house God intended for me.

The next morning, Larry arrived. Not being bold or an outspoken person, I felt uncomfortable asking him to call the Realtor first thing, but I did. "I can't explain it," I said. "Please reach out again about that house on Jefferson Lane."

Right there in the car, Larry placed the call. It went to voice-mail. I felt deflated. *That's that. I followed my prompting from God, but what good did it do?*

We toured eight properties, but none compared to the photos of the one listed on Jefferson Lane. I couldn't help but feel discouraged. That house was perfect; nothing else I'd seen remotely interested me. Worry bubbled up. I started to panic. *What if I can't find a place I like?* I felt like crying.

After dinner, Larry called. "The strangest thing happened," he said, a tone of awe in his voice. "The Realtor for the house on Jefferson Lane just called. The buyers were at the title company this morning when they discovered the homeowners' association doesn't allow large dogs. They were torn between the house and their Labrador, but just now decided. They've rescinded the offer. It's back on the market."

I jumped in the car and met Larry at the house. It was even more beautiful than it looked online. The moment I walked through the front door, I was convinced. Within the hour, we made an offer. It was accepted. Weeks later, that house on Jefferson Lane was mine.

I marveled at the situation. If the person who ended up buying my previous house had drawn up a contract six weeks earlier, when she said she would, the house on Jefferson Lane would have been under contract. What I thought was a delay was really God's perfect timing. It was as if God had been holding this house for me. While I had been worried and in a panic to find a place to live, God was already at work, getting my house ready at just the right moment.

GOD'S MYSTERIOUS WAYS: THE FEELING OF HOME

Deciding where we're going to live is huge. For some people, that can change many times over their lifetime. Others grow deep roots in a single community. Although God can use us anywhere as long as we're open to His direction, making choices about big moves can bring on a lot of anxiety. Here are some things that might help if you're in that situation.

- **Pray.** Ask for God's direction. Tell Him that you want to be where He wants you to be. That you want to do what He wants you to do. Then take the time to be still and listen to that quiet, inner voice that gives you peace beyond understanding.

- **Seek.** But then don't just sit there. There's an old adage that says it's easier to steer a moving car than a parked car. Do some research. Make a list of pros and cons that reflect your values, not just those things that seem better. For instance, one place might be slightly more expensive, but it puts you close to amenities that are important to you.

- **Act.** Take a step in one direction. Trust that God will keep giving you signposts. Stay in communication with Him about your trajectory and, instead of just asking Him to bless it, ask Him to clearly show the way.

- **Reflect.** Think about times that you have felt that true sense of peace about where you live. That long exhale that assures you you're in the exact right place. How can you experience that "this is home" feeling every time?

God Knew I Needed to Be There

Rebecca Hastings

*Commit to the LORD whatever you do, and
he will establish your plans.*

—PROVERBS 16:3 (NIV)

I gathered the papers I needed from the car and made a
mental note of the other errands I needed to do. My kids'
elementary school wasn't a typical middle-of-the-day stop,
but at the last minute, I had decided to bring in some paperwork I kept forgetting to send to school. I had other things on
my to-do list, all in the other direction, but for some reason as
I reached the end of my driveway, I made a snap decision to
head to the school first.

Standing at the door, I waited for the secretary to buzz
me in. The lock released, and I pushed open the door and
walked through the foyer, unprepared for what would
come next.

The principal was rushing toward the office when she saw
me. "How did you know to come in? Did the secretary call
you?" she said, making her way toward me and pulling me
toward the office.

A mix of panic and dread stirred inside me. *What is she talking about? Why did she need me to come in?* "I'm just here to drop something off," I offered, holding the papers up as evidence.

"Oh. Wow. OK. Come with me." She brought me through the busy office to the conference room. Before opening the door, she spoke quietly, "Everything is OK. Your daughter accidentally closed a door when her friend's hand was resting on the frame. Her friend will be all right, but there's an ambulance on the way. She is in a lot of pain and it was bleeding quite a bit. It was a complete accident."

I felt a wave of relief that my daughter was OK, and in hearing that her friend would be as well. I blew out a breath of air I didn't realize I was holding. "Where's my girl? Is she all right?"

"Yes. I mean, she's not hurt but she's upset. She's been crying, so we brought her down here. She's in here with the social worker." The principal gestured to the closed conference room. She paused and looked at me again, studying my face, "You really didn't know?"

"I had no idea. I wasn't even supposed to come in today. Just dropping something off."

"Well, that sure is something," she said, opening the door.

I met my seven-year-old's teary gaze and rushed to her, wrapping her in my arms. While she had been crying before, her tears came in a flood now, letting all that she tried to hold in release when she was safe in my arms. Her little body shook, overwhelmed with emotion. "I didn't mean to, Mommy. I didn't see her hand." The words tumbled out mixed with sniffles and hiccupping sobs.

"I know, baby. It was an accident." I held her, kneeling on the floor as the principal and social worker looked on.

"I was just telling her that," the social worker offered. "Accidents happen all the time. Your friend isn't mad. She's going to be OK," she reassured my daughter.

I continued to hold my girl, rubbing her back and trying to calm her down. I knew she was devastated at having hurt a friend. The words we offered were little comfort. Instead, I leaned against the wall, holding her in my lap. As she cried, I whispered a prayer over her.

The principal stepped out to coordinate the ambulance with the school nurse. Her friend was on her way to the hospital. When the principal returned, she shared that the girl's mom was with her and the ambulance crew had assured everyone the girl would be fine.

After a few minutes, the tears slowed. My girl looked up at me and whispered, "I'm glad you're here, Mommy."

The principal affirmed the sentiment. "That makes two of us." Looking directly at me, she asked again, "You really had no idea what was going on, did you?"

I shook my head.

"Well, I shouldn't be saying this, but the timing was just too perfect. God knew you needed to be here." She shook her head again before patting my daughter's back.

I had no plans to come to the school that day, but God guided me to show up at my daughter's school at the precise moment that she needed me. My daughter would have been fine if I hadn't come, but seeing me, feeling my arms around her, and letting me comfort her and pray for her made a devastated seven-year-old feel loved. God knew she needed that.

Whether running errands, making an unexpected stop, or simply changing plans, God directs our paths and our timing to be right where He wants us.

Two Jobs, One Day

Jessica Andrus Lindstrom

There are no mistakes, no coincidences; all events are blessings given to us to learn from.
—ELISABETH KÜBLER-ROSS

My son giggled as he looked up at me, waving his chubby little arms in the air. I finished pinning his diaper together and bent down to tickle his tummy again with a kiss. Another chortle came from his beaming face.

My husband appeared in the doorway and smiled.

"Daddy!" our one-year-old squealed with delight.

Tim bent down to pick up our son, kissing me on the cheek as he rose.

"You ready for your big day?" he asked.

"I guess so," was my tentative response. "But I'm nervous."

Before motherhood stepped in, I had worked full-time as an English teacher and college counselor. After the birth of my son, I had shifted to a part-time schedule. When Mrs. Arguello, the new head of the school, was hired shortly before the start of the last academic year, she had accepted my previously arranged part-time schedule without complaint. However, in recent weeks, she had been pressuring me to return to a full-time position. I hadn't yet signed a contract for the next school year, and we had scheduled a meeting for that morning to discuss whether I could still continue working part-time. I loved my job and wanted to keep it, but I wanted the time to watch my son grow up even more.

I sighed audibly, dreading the meeting and the difficult decision I might be forced to make. My husband patted my back.

"Buck up," he said. "You know in your heart where your priorities lie."

I nodded, though I still felt uneasy about lobbying for the part-time position I desired, sighing again as I went to get dressed.

Thirty minutes later, I drove down the road with the sweet smell of clover wafting through the open window, reflecting on my idyllic summer. The arts camp my school hosted each year had ended the day before, with many parents present for the final dramatic production my students had performed perfectly. My son watched the show from the back of the auditorium, sitting on the lap of the senior class member who had cared for him each day while I taught and directed my student thespians. He clapped along exuberantly during the curtain call and could be heard shouting "That's my mama!" when I appeared to bow with the cast.

Remembering his joyful outbursts, I laughed aloud despite my current concerns. *How blessed I am.*

Pulling into the school parking lot, I parked beside my supervisor's sedan. Before exiting the car, I paused and prayed, repeating the words I spoke each morning before I rose from bed. "Let the words of my mouth, the meditations of my heart, and the actions of my hands be acceptable to You today, O God, my strength and my redeemer."

The door to Mrs. Arguello's office was slightly ajar. I approached and tapped lightly.

"Come in," came her matter-of-fact response.

As I entered, she rose from the seat behind her desk and moved toward me.

"That was a charming play your students performed at the end of camp," she said, motioning me to take a seat in an armchair by the desk. "You certainly are a gifted teacher, and you're liked by so many of your students and their parents. I've been impressed with your organization and creativity."

"Thank you," I said, smiling up at her. "It pleases me that you were pleased."

She smiled back, picked up a folder, handed it to me, and then returned to the chair behind her desk.

"I know you have asked to remain part-time this year," she began, as I fingered the folder in my hands. "But I want our teaching staff to be full time, fully committed to all school activities and programs. One part-time teacher needs to be balanced with another, and the inquiries I receive almost daily from teachers looking for jobs are all requests for full-time employment. I am hoping you will accept a compromise."

She paused, watching me while I opened the folder.

"The contract you hold is a full-time contract," she continued. "But it has you slated to work in the office part-time instead of teaching during the school year and assuming a new role as the director of the summer school program next year. You would be able to work from home, hiring your staff and organizing the program ahead of time, but you would need to be on campus full-time during the summer months."

As she spoke, I scanned the contract inserted in the folder and saw her words confirmed. My apprehension grew. Not to teach but working full-time as an administrator all summer instead? My heart pounded. I knew I could not accept such terms. *Please, God, give me the words You want me to speak. Let me know what You want me to do.*

"Unfortunately, I cannot give you additional time to consider my offer," Mrs. Arguello continued. "I need to know now whether or not you will accept this contract."

Shaken but prayerfully calm, I spoke. "I thank you for offering me a way to remain at the school next year, but in all honesty, I cannot accept a non-teaching position that has me essentially working full-time during the summer months."

"So, you are not going to sign this contract?"

I shook my head.

"What will you do? I assume you need an income of some sort."

"I don't know which doors will open for me, as I have not looked for any other part-time employment. But I trust God has a plan for me I'm unaware of at this point."

"Good luck," Mrs. Arguello said crisply and rose to take the folder from my outstretched hand.

I had the distinct feeling that she knew when she created the position that I was not going to accept it. I sensed that, for some reason, she was relieved the meeting was over and that I was not returning. Unsettled, I rose from my chair, thanked her for her time, and left the office.

I drove home in a daze and, upon entering the house, told my husband I no longer had a job.

"It will be OK," he said encouragingly. "You've chosen your child over your career, and you know in your heart that decision is the right one."

I drove home in a daze and, upon entering the house, told my husband I no longer had a job.

"But is it? My income has paid many of our bills. What will we do to cover what I used to pay?"

"We'll make things work. It will be OK," Tim repeated.

I wasn't so sure, but when I slipped upstairs to peek at our son napping in his crib, my fears dissolved. I thanked God for the time I would have to spend with this child in the months to come.

Later that afternoon, while hanging diapers on the line to dry, I thought about how much I would miss teaching, how much I would miss the students and the camaraderie of colleagues I had known for the past ten years. I still wished something would miraculously materialize to keep my career as an educator on track, but, admittedly, I felt much more at peace now with my decision to stay home than I had an hour ago.

As I watched two squirrels chase each other playfully around the yard, I heard the landline ringing inside. A few moments later, Tim came to the screen door.

"There's someone on the phone who wants to talk with you," he said, his tone uncertain.

"Who is it?"

"I don't know. He didn't say."

I clamped a clothespin to the corner of the last diaper and went inside to answer the call.

"Hi," said a familiar voice.

It was John, a fellow English teacher who had left the school a year before to take a position as the senior editor for the publishing branch of an educational foundation in town. "I need a writer for a major project we are undertaking and thought of you. Would you, by any chance, have time to write?"

I couldn't believe my ears and felt goosebumps moving from my toes to my neck. "Would I be working in an office at the foundation?" I asked.

"No. You'd be writing from home. You would have deadlines to meet each month and would be paid per monthly assignment."

Warm tears came to my eyes. The timing was extraordinary. God had provided.

"Are you still there?" the voice spoke again.

"Yes, John. I am still here. A bit overwhelmed, but still here. I accept your offer with no hesitation. When do I begin?"

A Bite of Truth

Elsa Kok Colopy

He guides me along the right paths for his name's sake.
—Psalm 23:3 (NIV)

I like dogs, and dogs like me.

Or so I thought.

Everything changed one warm Saturday morning when I went for a walk with my husband and our dog. We walked a familiar route—left out of the house, across a main drag, down through a lovely neighborhood and circling back toward home. As we crossed the main road, we chatted away, laughing about one of our children and some teenage antics. Up ahead, a mixed-breed pup came jogging toward us. Our dog is pretty friendly, so they greeted one another with a sniff and a wag. I held out my hand to let him sniff me as well. "Hey boy, how are you?"

The strange dog sniffed my hand and must have so enjoyed the smell that he began to follow us. Brian and I kept talking, laughing about this and that, catching up on life. After we completed the full circle, I glanced back, and our new friend was still trotting behind.

"I don't know, babe," I said, "I'm a little worried about him. I don't want him to follow us across the main road." I urged my husband to walk up ahead with our dog, while I stayed behind to try and shoo the pup back to his home.

My plan seemed to be working. Brian walked on ahead, and the pup stayed by me. His eyes were fixed on mine. "Head on home, pup. It's time for you to go home." He had come from the houses nearby, so I waved my hand in that direction. "Go ahead, off you go!"

He kept his eyes on me and didn't move.

"Go on, boy! I don't want you to get hit by a car."

The next moment seemed to happen in slow motion. The oh-so-friendly pup leaned back on his haunches and launched himself toward me. My jaw dropped as my eyes widened. In a move of instinctive self-defense, I turned my body to try and

---

I was hiccupping and breathing quickly as I walked. "That dog . . . he . . . he bit me. . . . In the butt!"

---

deflect him. It didn't work. All my turn did was present him with a delectable human body part to chomp down upon.

I felt the sharp pain before I could do anything to save myself. The dog dropped to the ground and took off running. I couldn't believe it. I reached back to feel the tear in my jeans. "Ouch!" I stared dumbfounded as the dog ran away, leaving me holding my bum in my hand. "But I was nice to you!" I yelled.

I turned and began limping toward Brian. I was hiccupping and breathing quickly as I walked. "That dog . . . he . . . he bit me. . . . In the butt!"

Brian rushed over and gently helped me to hobble back to the house. As soon as we got home, we called the local sheriff. The last thing we wanted was for someone else to get bit.

The sheriff pulled into our driveway and we explained all that had happened. He was a typical southern gentleman, and he tipped his hat with an embarrassed nod as he told me the next step. "I'm sorry, ma'am," he drawled, "But we're going to have to take a picture of that."

Of course you are.

My husband ushered us all indoors to keep from offering additional fodder for the gawking neighbors. We preserved my dignity as best as we could, even as the sheriff documented the bite. Adding insult to injury, I also had to schedule a rabies shot, "just to be safe."

As I slowly healed, I remember praying to God and asking how such a situation could even remotely be His will. *Why, God?*

A few weeks later, my hubby and I wanted to go for another walk. There was no way we were going to head in the same direction, so we explored a bit and found a backwoods trail not too far from our house. As we walked, I was astounded that we had no idea this beautiful trail had been here the whole time. It had rolling hills, gorgeous trees, a babbling brook, and just enough squirrels for our pup to chase.

I remember walking one gorgeous afternoon and marveling at the light shining through the trees. As I looked up at the sky, a burst of laughter came from deep within. This was just so God. We had been talking to our teen about a relationship that had soured. We told her that oftentimes God allows pain in a situation because that might be the only way we let go and that He often has something far better around the corner. My dog bite experience had proven that out in the best of ways. It had taken the pain of a dog bite to lead us to somewhere far better—beyond what we had hoped could exist so close by.

A divine revelation. God knew. God saw. God had a plan.

And a good story to go with it.

The Envelope and Kenya

Tina Wanamaker

———✤———

God's will done in God's way will never lack God's supply.
—HUDSON TAYLOR

For the last three years the answer had been no. But a simple white rectangle made of paper helped to change the no to a yes.

Sister Elizabeth had been inviting me each year to come teach a women's conference in Kenya, and each year I had replied in the negative. I couldn't do it—yet. I had a feeling in my heart that the Lord wanted me to do it, but the timing had to be right. And so, I waited. I waited on the Lord for His answer and asked for His timing to be made clear.

The conference was in October each year. As usual, in early spring, Sister Elizabeth had invited me to come, but this time I didn't give her an outright no. In the past years I knew it wasn't time, but this year had a different feel to it. One part of that was that our four kids were older and more self-sufficient, and I wasn't feeling as concerned about leaving them. So I told Sister Elizabeth that we should seek the Lord together regarding this. I had been asking the Lord specifically to provide financially for my travel if it was His will for me to go.

Traveling to Kenya wasn't something that I had gone out looking to do. I hadn't even considered it until the invitation came the first year. The second year I considered it a bit more. I had been working with some ministry partners in that area, so I could potentially go to Narok to see how they were doing and find out what support they needed, then also teach at Sister Elizabeth's women's conference in Kisumu.

It seemed good and a little crazy too. I mean, what home-school momma traveled halfway around the world by herself? I figured that if the Lord was in it, it would all work out well and accomplish His purpose. But was He? Was God in it? Was it His timing for me to go this year? I kept bringing it before Him.

One day I received a phone call from a friend. She told me that she had something she wanted to give me and asked if we could meet. I said yes and joined her later that day in a parking lot. After we exchanged greetings, she took out a white envelope and held it in her hand. She explained that she had recently received an inheritance and had been praying about what God would have her do with it. She was going to pay this and take care of that. She also shared that she felt the Lord's leading to give me something for ministry as well.

My friend handed me the envelope and told me to use it as I felt led to. I took it, hugged and thanked her, and we parted ways. I got in my car and held the envelope in my hand. I felt so grateful to my friend. I thought about what a little bit could do to help in book distribution or a cover design or whatever the Lord would choose for me. I slowly opened the envelope to find a check inside addressed to me. My eyes rested on the amount. It was significantly more than I had expected.

As I sat there looking at that check a thought came to my mind: Kenya. This was God's provision to travel to Kenya. This is what I had been asking Him for. This was confirmation of His timing to go that fall. This was evidence that He saw, heard, and acted. My heart swelled with gratitude toward God. A smile spread across my lips.

I slowly opened the envelope to find a check inside addressed to me. My eyes rested on the amount. It was significantly more than I had expected.

I thought of my friend, who had no idea what had been on my mind and in my heart and on my lips in prayer. I had chosen not to share my thoughts about going to Kenya with anyone except my husband. I wanted it to be between me and God alone. I wanted to make sure it was Him and not someone wanting to help and be kind. And it was. It was all Him. He had prompted Sister Elizabeth to ask me to come. He had made the connection with the ministry partners. He had placed the desire to go in my heart. He had given my friend the thought and obedience to step out in faith and give. And He knew the perfect timing of all of it.

And so, that October was my first trip to Kenya. It was incredible, hard, faith building, stretching, and so much more. And that was just on my end! What He did in lives and hearts beside mine only He knows the fullness of. What I know is that Africa changed me. I'd like to think some folks in Africa were changed by that trip as well. I felt that God widened my heart and challenged me in my faith walk during that trip. I was put in situations where I had to find new ways to share with women I didn't know. He broadened my perspective and increased my trust. I leaned hard into the Lord and the leading of the Holy Spirit, and He granted me a wider perspective of Him, His grace, His mercy, and His heart toward people.

There were many times I didn't know what to do and asked the Lord for His leading and intervention. And of course, He showed up. Because that's what He does. He shows up, on time, and on His time. And sometimes He shows up with a dream to go to Kenya that you didn't know you had. And sometimes He throws in a white envelope or two for good measure. And you find that the dream and the envelope go hand in hand, because it was when I saw the envelope that I knew it was Him and not me; it was His thought and not mine. I needed that confirmation when some of the hard things came along—confirmation that was brought through an envelope handed to me by a friend.

GOD'S MYSTERIOUS WAYS: JUST WHAT WE NEED

It's not hard to imagine that if God hears everything that we say to Him, then He knows just how to connect people so they can provide for one another's needs. So when we're praying about a needed amount of money, or some other specific provision, it may seem amazing when someone arrives to fill that need, but to God it's just another day at work. And sometimes the need filled is so specific, and the timing so perfect, that we can feel His hand on us.

- **Pray.** Sometimes God's answers to prayer are not what we expect. He knows our needs, but He doesn't always provide for them in the way we think. Pray with an open heart, and be ready to look outside the box.

- **Seek.** In the Bible there's the story of a blind man named Bartimaeus. Jesus asked him what he wanted done for him. He very clearly said, "I want to see again." Search your heart to know what exactly it is you want God to do for you.

- **Act.** When God tells you something very specific— often through just a distinct impression in your heart—act on it. Maybe you're not the one in need, but the one through whom God will provide. As in our stories, you might not have any idea why you're giving someone something, but if God tells you to do it, do it.

- **Reflect.** How have you seen God provide exactly what you need in the past? How does that change how you respond to His promptings in your spirit now? Keep open communication with God for any opportunities He might have for you in the future.

When Obedience Became God's Defogger

Kristen Paris

"We must obey God rather than human beings!"

—ACTS 5:29 (NIV)

"If you go to church again, I'll change the locks on the doors."

It was the latest in a long line of threats my mother had made, trying to keep my budding Christian faith from taking me further down what she perceived as a dangerous road. I didn't want to disobey her—and since she and my father separated, there was no one else in the house to appeal to—but neither could I leave my Savior. He was the first person in my life who I knew loved me, and I clung to Him with everything my confused sixteen-year-old heart had.

Then, the day came. I'd stayed late at youth group to clean up, partly because my newfound joy bubbled up to overflowing in the community of God's people, but also because I didn't want to go home to screaming about how wrong I was to choose the impractical way of following Christ.

When I finally got home, I put my key in the lock as usual. But this time was different. The doorknob didn't turn. I was locked out.

A wave of fear hit me. What was I supposed to do? Where could I go? I panicked, but then my practical survivor instinct took over. I had friends, and I had the church. From a pay phone, I started calling the few numbers I had memorized until someone answered. They found me a temporary place to stay with a family from church. That didn't last, as my mother began threatening anyone who took me in. They did talk about adopting me, but I didn't want to infuriate my mother. I hoped and prayed for her salvation, and that we would subsequently share a deeper bond.

For months, I jumped from one temporary home to another. Each time one door closed, God opened a new one. Some offered longer-term options, until my mom called the police because these friends were "harboring a runaway." The fact that I'd been kicked out didn't seem to matter. So I slept on couches when I could, frequently asking my mom if I could come home. The answer was consistent. I could return as soon as I left the church.

That was the deal. If I walked away from Jesus, my house key would work again.

But I knew that God was giving me a new key—unlocking my trembling heart to a life of deeper faith.

Eventually, space opened up in a house shared with four girls. It wasn't an easy way to live. Work piled on top of school, leaving little time for anything else. But I was strong. I could do this—or so I thought.

My roommate worked at a snack bar, living on discarded treats that had passed their expiration. An off-brand pancake mix was my staple. Two other women in the house worked for a ministry and did a little better. A final housemate was only fifteen, so the older girls looked after her needs. We struggled, but got by.

I worked at three different stores, all under the same manager. Increasingly, my shifts were confined to the least desirable of the three—a T-shirt shop. It was a tiny kiosk in an obscure corner of an outdoor shopping mall, manned by one person at a time. Alone, surrounded by decals with images of marijuana leaves and mostly crude sayings, I tried to shrink

---

The city below had disappeared, as though there were nothing in the world but myself and that cross.

---

to invisibility. We printed custom T-shirts, which deepened my discomfort into shame and fear. The words I printed stood in stark contrast to all that was good, pure, lovely, and praiseworthy. If Jesus walked through those doors, I knew His eyes would hold tears. But I had bills to pay; what else could I do?

I requested a move from the Shirt Shack to the Coffee Merchant. My request was denied. I felt stuck. Desperate, I applied to nearly every other store in the mall. Weeks passed, with only a single interview.

One sleepless night, I tossed and turned. Finally giving up on sleep in the early morning, I dressed, grabbed my Bible, and slipped outside into a dense fog. I drove to a quiet place to cry my heart out to God. There was a park at the top of a hill with a cross that stood as its focal point. I curled up on a low wall not far from the cross. Below, the city was covered in fog, while light from the rising sun painted the top of the fog in shades of gold and pink. The city below had disappeared, as though there were nothing in the world but myself and that cross. I wished it was real, that I need not return to the world now obscured from view. Warmed by sunlight, I still felt miserable, knowing I couldn't stay on the mountaintop.

"Lord, what should I do? My work is offensive. The leers from the men watching me just add to the shame I feel while pressing their rude, graphic slogans onto their shirts. But how can I quit? It's also wrong for me to walk out on my responsibilities. My car needs gas. I need food. The utilities, car insurance, and rent have to be paid. It's hard enough with my job; without it, it would be impossible. Father, you know I'm trying to find other work, but nothing has come through."

I poured out my pain and worry in prayer. I didn't have answers, but I knew He did. "Lord, wherever you want me, I will follow. But I don't know what to do. I pretend to be strong and resourceful, but you know I'm not. I'm scared. Direction, please?" Comforting silence hugged me, taking the edge off my confusion. My mind and soul quieted until I felt empty. Not a bad emptiness. Just a deep, deep stillness. In the silence, a word formed. *Quit.*

That's it? Just quit? I couldn't! It made no sense. Walking out on my responsibility ran contrary to every principle I'd been raised by. But it didn't sound like a suggestion. Leaving my job was no longer a decision to be made. It was, at that moment, the only path I could take to follow my Savior. And I knew I couldn't wait any longer.

Tears welled up and then spilled over. Would I have to sleep on a park bench or eat from garbage cans? What about my safety—wasn't that more important than the trashy, vulgar words I was printing? I must have heard wrong. Maybe my desire to get out of the situation was prompting this thought. "Am I hearing you right, God? Just quit?"

You heard correctly—quit.

As tears continued trickling down, I waited, hoping God would go easy on me and give me a more reasonable way out. Maybe quit as soon as another job came through? That's what I was already planning anyway.

I love you, daughter. Come, follow me. *I didn't hear the words aloud, but the answer was no less clear than if it had been written on the wall.*

Now!

It sounded crazy. But I'd committed to follow Jesus at any cost—not just when I felt I was ready. I'd assumed I'd be an adult before being faced with tough choices. But apparently, God was calling me to a life of crazy faith. Not when I was old enough, educated enough, or strong enough. Here and now.

I love you, daughter. Come, follow me. I didn't hear the words aloud, but the answer was no less clear than if it had been written on the wall. God was shining light on the next step of my path. The fact that I was petrified didn't release me from the command. He wasn't giving me the option to delay until I'd found a safe way to follow Him. He was my safe way.

Was this where following God led? To danger and home-lessness? Tears flooded down until I was exhausted, but at peace. I felt a subtle confidence in the decision to follow my Creator, even when His instruction didn't make sense. God knew me, and He had spoken.

So I surrendered. "OK, God, I'll do it your way. Please hold me. Whatever lies ahead, don't leave me." Numb now to the consequences I feared, I lay back on the wall, soaking in the sunshine. Peace soaked into my soul just as the sun's rays soaked into my skin.

When I finally returned to my car, more words pushed their way into my mind. *As you drive down into the fog, your mind will also become foggy and confused. Hold on to what I've told you. Hold on to Me.*

Sure enough, as I reentered the fog, doubt haunted me. Could I really give up my means of support? Maybe I was deluding myself. Surely God wouldn't want me to live on the streets. There had to be a better way. I'd simply wait a bit. That would be the responsible thing to do, right?

I knew those thoughts were leading me in the wrong direction. God had spoken, and I couldn't ignore Him.

The distance from my car to my boss's office seemed horribly long, but too short at the same time. I questioned my own sanity with each step. But God's command had been firm and clear.

I quit, hoping my reasons came across respectfully but clearly. Then, I worried. *What now?* I drove home tortured by doubts.

Flopping onto my bed, face down, I listened to the clock tick. Out of the corner of my eye, a slip of paper on my nightstand caught my attention. There was a message. I called the scrawled number. That one interview had paid off. I had a job offer at a department store. I could start immediately. It even came with a pay raise!

God had my back. He knew that job was already waiting for me even before He told me to quit the old one. Why hadn't He waited? I would have quit as soon as I had the new job. But I would have been relying on myself. Instead, God taught me the value of obedience in a way I'd never forget.

Lessons of the heart don't come easily to me. I prefer to live in the world of intellect and theory, guarding my heart so well that even the best things in life often get locked out. Maybe that's why God pushed me to act against logic. Perhaps the knowledge that perfect love casts out fear was one I personally would learn best if I first experienced fear. Without panic, I might have had no opportunity to practice radical faith. And then I would have missed out on the deep peace of trusting my heavenly Father for a future He could see while I could not.

But God loves me too much for that. He gently called me to step off a cliff just so I could experience His arms catching me.

Obedience was the defogger God used to clear my vision.

God's GPS: Recalculating to Tamale

Amy Hagerup

In their hearts humans plan their course,
but the Lord establishes their steps.

—Proverbs 16:9 (NIV)

"We're home!" my three children called out as they scrambled out of our friend's blue sedan after their morning at the international school. Our children had spent the majority of their young years in Ghana. When we'd moved there eleven years ago, our oldest kids were two-and-a-half years and eight months old. Our third child was born in town four months after our arrival and came home to our stucco ranch house. Ghana had become home to us. Speaking the local language was second nature, and we had recently seen a fourth church start up in one of the nearby villages as the local mission work prospered.

Recently, we had hosted a single missionary, Kevin, who ministered in the upper region of Ghana. To reach our home in Kumasi, a city in the south, he'd had to drive through the city of Tamale, where our mission had established a small presence to help in planting churches.

As he sprawled out on our sofa, Kevin lamented some of the hardships of life in Tamale: electricity was spotty, and tanks of water had to be delivered to homes. The weather there was hot, dry, and dusty. "Tamale is the armpit of Ghana!" Kevin declared. "Pray that you are never assigned there."

I wasn't too concerned about Kevin's dire report. We had no plans to move. Relocating to northern Ghana would require learning another language and establishing new relationships for church planting. Our children would have to leave behind our stable home environment, the international school they had grown to love, and a beautiful group of international friends. Life in Kumasi had become our heartbeat; surely we were planted for the long haul.

⁘

The time came for furlough—a temporary return to the US to reconnect with our family and culture, as well as to share in churches about our ministry. For my husband to continue working on his masters in missions at Columbia International University (CIU), we planned to spend the academic year in South Carolina. After arriving, we moved into our furnished rental home and got the kids enrolled in their schools while Mark adjusted to life as a graduate student at the university.

Prayer days were a refreshing monthly occurrence at CIU. Because these days were dedicated to prayer, regular classes were canceled and an esteemed preacher spoke in chapel. On the first prayer day of the school year, Mark listened attentively as the speaker wrapped up his message. He whispered into the microphone: "Are you willing to do anything for the Lord? Go anywhere the Lord calls you? Anywhere?"

Ushers shuffled down the aisles, handing out stacks of small commitment cards to be distributed down each row. The speaker continued, "Take this, pray over it, and sign it with your response." The card, which was intended to be kept by each individual as a reminder of their commitment, had three options: pray for missions, give to missions, and go wherever the Lord leads.

I stood still, a jolt of shock rippling through me. Us? Move to Tamale?

During his private prayer time, my husband studied that little card. He told the Lord that all three choices had been active in our lives for many years. We had lived in seven different places on the mission field: six in Ethiopia, where we started our married life, and Kumasi in Ghana, our current location. That was where we had been the longest.

Mark sighed, but spoke decisively as he finished his prayer: "I want to renew my commitment to go anywhere You want us to go. Amy and I will move again if that is Your plan for us."

Mark checked off all three options, signed the yellow card, and tucked it into the pages of his Bible.

An hour later, he returned home to find a letter in the mailbox from our director in Ghana. "That's interesting. Why would Isaac be sending us a letter?" Mark muttered as he fingered the envelope. He plopped onto the floral sofa, pushing the throw pillows to the side.

Tearing the flap, he extricated the thin white paper as I watched over his shoulder, silently reading about missionary colleagues retiring. Our director's letter continued, "Their departure will leave Tamale without any missionaries from our organization. I believe you would be a good fit for taking over that ministry. Would you be willing to move to Tamale when you return to Ghana after your furlough?"

Mark's eyes widened as he sucked in a quick breath. "Amy, you won't believe this, but I just signed a commitment card after chapel today saying that we would be willing to move anywhere God wanted us to go!"

I stood still, a jolt of shock rippling through me. *Us? Move to Tamale? The armpit of Ghana?*

Once the truth of the situation began to sink in, a wave of calm washed over me. A few hours ago, God had spoken clearly to my husband during chapel. He had known this life-changing letter was on its way, and He had already planned for the change in ways we didn't yet know.

There are no random turns in a believer's journey when it comes to God's guidance—it's like we have a divine GPS. This was an unmistakable recalculating of our ministry location.

We said yes.

⁓⟫⟫⟫⟫⟫⟫⟫⁓

At the end of the school year, we returned to Ghana, and a few months later, we moved to Tamale. As we drove into our new town, I couldn't help but notice the brown, dusty landscape stretching out before me. My stomach tightened as I took in our change of location. The only bursts of color came from the faded cloths wrapped around the women's bodies. While a few multistory buildings dotted the area, they were nothing like the apartment complexes and market structures we had left behind in Kumasi. Tamale felt different, but we were up to the challenge of learning to thrive in our new place of God's assignment.

Finally, we pulled up to the closed gate of our rental home.

God blessed us with next-door neighbors, Jordan and Lisa, who became our co-laborers in spreading the Gospel. Jordan had a mega-vision for building God's kingdom in Tamale and the surrounding villages, and Mark and Jordan jumped into their work right away.

My bond with Lisa happened almost overnight: we studied the Bible together, cooked in each other's kitchens, and shared the Gospel with the girls in the sewing class that she taught. Our blossoming friendships overpowered the inconvenience of electricity shortages and water supply challenges (which lessened over time). Tamale living started to flourish in our lives.

꧁꧂

During our nine years in Tamale, we saw seven churches planted, with many men and women being discipled. Sadly, we also experienced a tribal conflict where many villages were burned. Mark and others assisted with the relief aid offered to the refugees. Along with physical resources, he and his team shared spiritual food.

After settling into our church work, I looked for a ministry my teenage daughters could participate in that didn't require knowledge of the tribal language. An acquaintance introduced me to the local orphanage, and my teens and I began to go there once a week to play with the orphans and teach Bible stories to the children at the nursery school.

As God would have it, we fell in love with a tiny orphaned newborn and brought her to our home for a visit—something the orphanage administrators encouraged. That infant girl, who we named Kinza, was awarded to us in court as our child four months later. When Kinza was three years old, God brought Colette, a motherless toddler, into our lives and hearts. We were also able to adopt her into our growing family.

Of course we had hoped for spiritual fruit when we moved from Kumasi to the "undesirable" Tamale. But we had no idea that our obedience to God would lead us not only to the joy of spiritual births but also to the delight of welcoming two new children into our family!

Trusting God's GPS not only guides us to His spiritual destinations, but also to the blessings He bestows upon us along the way, even if the journey takes an unexpected detour.

Show Us the Money

Cecil Taylor

❧ ——————————— ❧

*"Can you fathom the mysteries of God? Can
you probe the limits of the Almighty?"*

—JOB 11:7 (NIV)

E ven after the birth of two sons, my wife, Sara, and I felt
like our family picture was incomplete. During our five
years of infertility, our hearts had opened to the idea
of adoption, but we couldn't figure out how to get it done.

From the time our boys were old enough to understand, we
told them that our family would eventually expand through
adoption. Sometimes we would search online for groups of
siblings to adopt through a state agency, hoping to keep them
together in our family. Other times, we would investigate international adoptions or domestic adoptions through a private
agency. But nothing ever felt right. We prayed for guidance.

Then one Sunday, missionaries from China visited our
church. As Sara sat with the choir and I managed the boys
in the pew, the missionaries described the plight of girls in
China. At the time, parents were limited by China's one-child
policy, and many parents preferred a boy that would take care
of them in old age according to cultural norms. Kind parents
would abandon girls, hoping they might be adopted; other

parents simply dumped female infants in the river to experience a swift, cruel death.

As the missionaries spoke of Chinese orphanages overflowing with girls, Sara's eyes locked with mine. We knew this was the right opportunity for us.

Any adoption would cost substantial money, but an international adoption cost even more. Medical bills and other calamities had impacted our financial reserve, but we were determined, and we started saving.

After a year, our savings account held perhaps $500. Every time we contributed a worthwhile amount, we would have to draw it out again for an emergency or an unforeseen circumstance.

The next year, the missionaries returned to tell their story again. Once more, we dedicated ourselves to adopting a Chinese orphan. Once again, we couldn't manage to stash any significant cash. It looked like our adoption dream would end. The boys were getting older, farther away from a younger sister. We needed to act soon if we would add to our family so that our new daughter could interact with her brothers in a relatively close age range.

We had prayed before, but now our prayers became bold and specific: "Lord, our hearts are open, and we're willing to adopt, but things keep preventing us from saving. It doesn't seem like we can store up the money to do this. If it is Your will for us to become adoptive parents, then show us the money!"

We felt peaceful, knowing that whatever happened, the matter was now in God's hands. Yet we were still surprised by the way God's fingerprints appeared on what happened next and on a sequence of events throughout the adoption process.

God indeed showed us the money. At my high-tech job, I received a promotion and a significant, far-beyond-expectations salary increase. In consecutive quarters, I was given a sizable bonus, which was highly unusual because bonuses were only given annually. We felt the momentum building toward our goal. Then Sara's aunt succumbed to a long bout with cancer and left an unexpected inheritance for Sara that could be used toward our plan. Within six months of praying "show us the money," we had the amount needed for the adoption.

"Well, God delivered," I said. "I guess we need to go through with this!"

As Sara and I talked through the unprecedented string of events that had answered our prayer, all we could do was look at each other. "Well, God delivered," I said. "I guess we need to go through with this!"

God didn't just send us money but provided in other ways. Just as we were wondering what to do next, an agency specializing in Chinese adoptions held an information session at our church. We took our sons with us to the session, wanting them to be a part of the process from the start. When we arrived and realized that we were the only family that attended, we felt like God had arranged the session just for us. We met parents with adopted daughters and heard their stories. We learned the many precise steps that must be followed with the Chinese government. We decided to commit and put down the first sum of money toward the adoption process.

What we didn't know at the time was that half a world away, in that same month we committed, an eighteen-month-old girl was left on the streets on her own. She eventually landed in an orphanage with hundreds of other girls, one of about one hundred such orphanages in her city. God's match-making was underway to bring us together.

The agency's social worker visited our home multiple times to interview us about the ways we were raised and how we parented our sons. From the social worker's demeanor, we were sure we had no chance. But she wrote a glowing report and approved us to go forward.

We began building an extensive paper trail for the Chinese government, including birth certificates, marriage license, medical evaluations, employment letters, financial statements, background checks, and more. That was plenty to collect on its own, but the Chinese government required each document to be created in a certain way unfamiliar to most document providers. We had to explain carefully what we needed. Providers took extra time to generate and send us the papers in the necessary format.

Retaining a lawyer specializing in China adoptions proved crucial. After four months of gathering documents, we met, and she praised our thoroughness. Then she gently broke the bad news: each document had to be notarized, certified, and authenticated. In the detailed instructions from the adoption agency, the authentication step was missing. We had to tackle the paperwork collection a second time.

Four months later, we met again. Our lawyer informed us of another delay; China had just changed the requirements for some paperwork, so we had to request certain documents a third time. Ten months after we started, we finally secured the right documentation.

You might think Sara and I would be frustrated with all the setbacks and redoing of our previous work, but we believed that every delay was intended to put us together with the right daughter and sister for our family.

When we submitted the package to China in January 2001, we requested a girl in the age range of three to five years. We felt this would be the best fit, as the boys were six and nine at the time.

Then we waited and waited. We knew it could take anywhere from five months to two years to get approved, with no notice of progress. In the meantime, we prepared a bedroom for our daughter. Sometimes we would sit on her bed, look at the toy box and the shelves laden with books, and dream about her arrival.

Just days before Christmas, the adoption agency informed us we had a match. What a thrilling Christmas gift! We also received a letter from the orphanage, written in Mandarin and translated by our Chinese-speaking neighbor. The letter gave way too few details about our future daughter, but it contained her picture, so now we had a face to love.

We followed the agency's advice and sent a care package ahead that included toys and a photo album of our family. Our neighbor helped us annotate each picture in Chinese so the orphanage nannies could show our future daughter the family and home she would soon join.

The agency arranged for us to travel with other adopting families. In February 2002, nearly two years after we laid down the first payment to initiate adoption, Sara and I took our two sons with us to China to bring their sister home.

Before traveling, we had arranged for a dozen family members and friends to pray for us and receive our adoption progress email updates. Throughout the entirety of the trip, I experienced something I've never felt before or since—a sensation like I was moving within a cloud of prayer. It wasn't until we returned home that I learned those dozen people had forwarded our emails to more than 300 people who prayed daily for us. I didn't know that fact, but I could feel it. God's fingerprints again.

Throughout the entirety of the trip, I experienced something I've never felt before or since—a sensation like I was moving within a cloud of prayer.

Once we synchronized with our guide in China, we received unexpected news: through fortunate circumstance, we were allowed to visit the orphanage to pick up our daughter, whom we would name Rebecca. That visit created a memorable introduction to now three-and-a-half-year-old Rebecca, who seemed to recognize us from the photo album.

The first step of a multi-day process to extract her from China was taking her from the orphanage to a government office for official pictures. While the photographer snapped our first portrait as a family, Sara and I noticed the female workers in the government office pointing and clearly talking about us. We asked our guide what they were saying.

The guide responded, "They're talking about how so many girls come through here who don't want to be with their new family. Sometimes they protest so violently that the family has to take them back to the orphanage. Other times, the match just looks like a bad fit. But they said, with this group, you look like a family already!"

That first photo of our completed family is a prized possession. In my mind, our matchmaker had posted that picture on heaven's refrigerator well in advance, knowing the beautiful family completion that God would arrange.

My Little Fleece

Terrie Todd

*Gideon said to God, "If you will save Israel by my hand as
you have promised—look, I will place a wool fleece on the
threshing floor. If there is dew only on the fleece and all the
ground is dry, then I will know that you will save Israel
by my hand, as you said." And that is what happened.
Gideon rose early the next day; he squeezed the fleece and
wrung out the dew—a bowlful of water. Then Gideon said
to God, "Do not be angry with me. Let me make just one
more request. Allow me one more test with the fleece, but
this time make the fleece dry and let the ground be covered
with dew." That night God did so. Only the fleece was dry;
all the ground was covered with dew.*

—JUDGES 6:36–40 (NIV)

I was ready to leave home at thirteen.

Don't misunderstand. I wasn't what you'd typically
think of as a troubled kid. I entertained no intentions of
running away. I knew my parents loved me and I loved them.

School, not so much. Though I did all right academically,
I found it hard to grow as a Christian or to resist the pull of
the world around me. I wanted so much more. Our pastor's
daughter and my good friend, Sharon, two years my senior,

had enrolled in a Christian boarding school called Sunshine Bible Academy, five hundred miles from home. Her mother, an alumna of the school, had grown up in central South Dakota where Sunshine still stands, welcoming students from all over since the early 1950s. Its motto has always been "God's Truth for Today's Youth."

I'd observed Sharon blossom in her first two years. When she returned home for summers and Christmas, she shared stories of her adventures. The gospel team to which she belonged visited our church, promoting the school in stories and song. When they hung out with our youth group, I heard about what sounded like a delightful prospect. I wanted more than anything to enjoy dorm life, to have Christian teachers and classmates. To have the chance to sing in the choir and take classes our little public school couldn't offer.

Unfortunately, such a move wasn't in the cards for me. As the youngest of five children, I alone remained at home. My two sisters had married, and my two brothers had recently moved out to begin their adult lives. My parents weren't ready to face what we now call empty nest syndrome. I lost count of the times I heard my dad say, "We're so glad we still have our baby at home." How could I break my father's heart by announcing that I wished to go off to boarding school? It wasn't like we could FaceTime each day or even email. This was the 1970s. We'd be exchanging old-fashioned, snail-mail letters and once-a-month phone calls placed collect.

Other questions plagued me, too. How much did room, board, and tuition cost? Could my parents afford it? Added to those expenses would be fuel for making the thousand-mile round trip two or three times a year. Also, we lived in

Canada and were Canadian citizens. What paperwork might be involved?

Another minor detail bothered me. My mother was our local high-school principal. How might it affect her if some critic began gossiping about our little school not being good enough for the principal's kid? How would that look? What might people say?

I just couldn't do it.

I said nothing, but I couldn't forget about it. All through seventh grade, I imagined myself going off to Sunshine, having so many Christian friends, wearing the required skirts and dresses instead of jeans like I did at home. Sure, they'd have stricter rules and regulations than I was subject to at home, but for me the advantages seemed to outweigh everything. The more I tried to stop thinking about Sunshine Bible Academy, the more convinced I became that I wanted this. Did God want it for me, too? How could I tell?

Eighth grade came and the clock ticked. I'd learned to follow Jesus as a small child. The Bible stories I'd learned at Sunday school, Bible camp, and vacation Bible school encouraged me to trust God. Believing I could talk to Him about anything, I decided to pray about this schooling situation. Knowing the story of Gideon setting out a fleece to seek God's guidance, I prayed: "Lord, You know how much I want to go to Sunshine. But I'm afraid to approach Mom and Dad. They keep saying how happy they feel to still have me around. How can I do this to them? How do I even know if this is Your will for me? God, if You want me to go, please let them be the ones to bring it up. I'm not going to say a word. If they don't, I'll accept that staying here is Your plan."

Though my words may sound like quite the faith-filled prayer for a fourteen-year-old, I felt certain I'd be staying home and kissing my dreams goodbye. I figured the odds of Mom and Dad broaching the subject matched those of Gideon's fleece staying dry while the ground surrounding it glistened with dew. I kept quiet, consoling myself with the idea that at least I wouldn't need to drum up the courage for this huge step.

"God, if You want me to go, please let them be the ones to bring it up. I'm not going to say a word."

Then, one unseasonably warm January day, my mother and I went for a walk after school at her invitation. That never happened. It might be the *only* time it ever happened, given that I normally arrived home from school long before Mom. I still remember the melting snow and the enticing sunshine as we walked along the main drag of our little Manitoba town.

Then Mom said something that seemed not only out of character but completely out-of-the-blue to me. "How would you like to go to Sunshine next year?"

I was floored to learn that she and Dad had already been discussing the idea. They had perceived my unhappiness and wanted more for me as well. I had underestimated both their willingness to hear from God and God's ability to change hearts. I'm convinced He led them to this idea without my help. Of course, I said yes to going to Sunshine.

The next eight months were filled with anticipation as I prepared for this major change. I remember packing a small trunk with clothing, towels, bedding, toiletries, school supplies, and the electric hair rollers I'd received for Christmas. The nights leading to departure day found me sleepless with excitement.

While those first weeks in my new environment proved an adjustment, I still consider the four years I spent at Sunshine Bible Academy the single most formative period of my life. Whether my initial prayer revealed bold faith or timid cowardice, I'm still not sure. I only know God heard the cry of my fourteen-year-old heart and blessed me beyond measure. I grew in ways I simply would not have otherwise, developing tight friendships and self-confidence as I matured in my faith.

Not only did I make lasting friendships, but I met my future husband there—he graduated in the class one year ahead of me. He and I recently attended a forty-fifth reunion with many of the lifelong friends we made in high school. As we reminisced, laughed, prayed, hugged, cried, and worshiped God together, we shared many stories of trusting God throughout our lives and finding Him completely trustworthy and faithful. I couldn't help thinking of the young girl who'd trusted God for guidance by putting out a simple fleece—and of a good God who honored that trembling step of faith.

GOD'S MYSTERIOUS WAYS: ASKING FOR A SIGN

In Judges 6, Gideon asked God for a very specific sign: make this sheepskin wet and the rest of the ground dry. And when that happened, Gideon asked again, make this sheepskin dry and the ground all around it wet. He wasn't afraid to ask God twice to verify what Gideon was to do.

Sometimes when we're looking for answers, God gives us arrows. He shows us the path we're to walk even if the end is not yet in sight.

- **Pray.** Pray a bold prayer asking God to give you something tangible to let you know you're on the right track. It won't offend Him. But be open to Him speaking in a way you don't expect.

- **Seek.** Jesus often asked people, "What do you want me to do for you?" Read some of the stories from Mark 10 and Luke 18. Ask yourself exactly what it is you want God to do for you. Don't be surprised if it doesn't happen right away. God rarely works on our timetable, but He's also not in the business of confusing us. Our misunderstandings often stem from our impatience.

- **Act.** If you sense a clear direction from God, be bold and follow it—even if the guidance you receive isn't what you expected.

- **Reflect.** As you wait on God's arrows, spend quiet time in communion with Him. Let Him soothe your soul as He continues to work out His good and perfect plan.

An Extra Special Christmas Bonus

Felicia Harris-Russell

For God has not given us a spirit of fear, but of power and of love and of a sound mind.

—2 TIMOTHY 1:7 (NKJV)

My husband and I are blessed to own a small cleaning business that serves both residential and commercial clients. Our motto is "Excellence in Cleaning," and we put our hearts and souls into our work, not just our physical bodies.

When we started this business, I came to understand more deeply that venturing into entrepreneurship requires faith, courage, and the ability to overcome the fear of failure, the fear of rejection, and the fear of loss. I had to confront these challenges head-on, or I would fail before I even began.

To launch this wonderful business, we used money from our savings. We understood that if this ship began to sink, we wouldn't have a parent company or even a wealthy relative or friend that we could call to bail us out. What we did and still do have, though, is something far more valuable—faith in a God who is all-sufficient and not limited by our physical or financial resources. From the very beginning, we dedicated this enterprise to Him and asked Him to use it for His glory. Jesus is our anchor and our CEO.

Because our business is still growing, every new account we acquire, no matter its size, is precious to us. We don't disregard small accounts, because providing excellent service to micro accounts can lead to more lucrative opportunities in the future.

Since it takes much time, effort, and energy to win new accounts, we do everything in our power to keep them. So, if we must terminate an account, it's a serious matter.

Last year, I faced a significant dilemma when I had to decide whether to terminate one of my commercial accounts. The people were friendly, but they increasingly violated the payment terms of our contract. Even after I reminded them of their obligations, the violations continued for several months.

It was a small account, but we relied on it to help pay our bills. Additionally, the company I was considering terminating was linked to one of our other commercial clients. I was concerned that the connected company would cancel their services in protest if we terminated the account. If they did, we would end up losing two accounts instead of one, which meant a bigger financial hit on our bank account.

Anxiety about the possible consequences began to overwhelm my thoughts and disturb my peace. I needed to consult my CEO, Jesus, regarding what to do. To cancel or not to cancel was the question, and I prayed for weeks, seeking a clear answer.

I sensed the Lord guiding me to terminate the contract and trust Him to make up the difference in our monthly budget. I finally resisted the fear and surrendered to the leader of my heart. I submitted a notice of termination to the company.

One week after I gave notice of termination in December, we received a Christmas bonus from another customer. When I counted the cash gift that was inside the cheerful Christmas card, I was stunned. First my jaw dropped, and then my lips began to praise God while my feet started dancing with joy.

The envelope held an odd cash amount—$390. Why would they choose to give us exactly that much? I couldn't know what was in the minds of the people who gave us the bonus, but I did know that what they gave us was the exact monthly charge for the account we had just terminated. God had just sent us a clear sign: I had moved forward with faith in His leading, and He sent us this promise that not only did He have the next month covered, but that we were held in His hands, and He would keep our growing business safe.

God blessed us to the point that we had to turn away business. He made up for the lost income, and the connected account remained our very satisfied customer.

This experience not only boosted my faith but made me realize, more than ever, that it truly pays to include God in every business decision.

How God Extended My Timeline

Laura Bailey

The one who calls you is faithful, and he will do it.
—1 Thessalonians 5:24 (NIV)

My fingers lingered over the "request more information" button. I desperately wanted to learn more about the master's program in counseling on this college's website. This wasn't my first visit to the site: I'd scanned the programs, courses, and learning avenues numerous times, and practically had the offerings memorized. What could it hurt to submit my email, talk to a representative about the counseling courses, and better understand the time commitment?

I knew in my heart, though, that as much as I desired to become a professional counselor, now was not the time. I'd recently graduated from seminary, and the impact on my family's time and financial resources was still fresh. While my husband fully supported my desire to continue my theological and professional experience, he gently encouraged me to wait a year or two before enrolling.

Truthfully, I knew that in this season, taking on another two- or three-year commitment of late nights and early mornings wasn't the best decision for my family or me. Reluctantly, I clicked out of the web browser, shut the laptop, and headed to the nursery to wake my youngest daughter up from her nap. As I buried my head deep in her curls, breathed in her sweet baby smell, and soaked in her warm embrace, I felt peace about my decision. One day, my daughters would be older, my schedule more flexible, and perhaps the door would open back up for me to return to school.

As life has a way of doing, five years passed in a blink, and I once again lingered over the "request more information" button on the college's website. The desire to counsel women was still very much aflame in my heart, but I wasn't sure that this was the path the Lord wanted me to take. After speaking with my husband, I once again decided to pause this dream and wait for the Lord to give me a clear direction.

A few months later, I received an email from the pastor at my church, where I led the women's ministry. "I thought you would be a good fit for this," he wrote, sharing that a company in the area was looking for someone to fill an opening for a workplace chaplain.

A workplace chaplain? I thought chaplains were only in hospitals, the military, or called in during emergencies. As I scanned the requirements, I dismissed the idea that I would be a good fit for the role. I'd never counseled people in a professional setting before; my only related experience was in the women's ministry or talking on the couch with a friend. *Who would ever hire me for a position like this?* I thanked my pastor for his consideration and deleted the email.

But afterward, I found I couldn't stop thinking about the position. I felt a strong nudge to apply, and after wrestling with it for a few days, I submitted my résumé, assuming that would be the end of it. Less than an hour later, the company's owner called and asked if I could come for an interview.

When the appointed day arrived, I put on my best interview outfit and nervously went to meet the company owner at a local deli. He greeted me warmly, immediately calming my nerves.

"So, tell me what you know about being a workplace chaplain," he began.

"Well, truthfully, not too much," I responded bashfully. *What was I thinking, applying for a job like this?*

As I scanned the requirements, I dismissed the idea that I would be a good fit for the role. . . . Who would ever hire me for a position like this?

He shared more about his history, the company, and the job specifics. The company was one that contracted with local businesses to provide chaplain services, so I might be assigned to any one of a number of different places with different needs. As he finished outlining the position, he paused and looked at me directly. "So what do you think? Would you like to join us?"

Wait, what? Did he just offer me the job? I had barely even known what a chaplain did before the interview.

Seeing my shock, he smiled. "You know Mrs. Lucy."

"Oh yes, Mrs. Lucy. She is such a blessing." Mrs. Lucy was a pastor's wife in our community who I'd befriended a few years back when my children attended their church's preschool.

She exuded joy with her inviting personality and contagious smile. I didn't know that she had served as a chaplain, but I wasn't surprised.

It turned out that when the company owner saw on my résumé that I was from the same town as Mrs. Lucy, he reached out to her on the off chance she might know me. "She provided such a glowing recommendation that I feel comfortable offering you this job—if you want to move forward with it."

I accepted the offer on the spot, and I was amazed to learn that their current opening was for a staffing company. I'd spent ten years in the recruiting and job placement industry, so I knew this type of work and its challenges well.

I couldn't stop smiling as I drove home, my heart overflowing with gratitude. This was not how I had envisioned entering the counseling world, and the timeline was significantly extended, but now I understood that the Lord had a plan all along. While I did have a background in theology and staffing that would help me in this new role, on the surface, it didn't make sense that the company would offer the job to me, someone with no direct experience as a chaplain. Only God could receive the credit for this divinely orchestrated series of events, and all I could do was say "yes," walking in faith through the opportunity he provided.

I am happy to report that I am thoroughly enjoying my new role. Last week, I was asked if I would take an additional chaplain assignment! I haven't released the idea of returning to school, but I am learning to trust in God's timing. God's plan and purpose are always better than my own.

Let's Talk Colorado

Elsa Kok Colopy

❦————◦————❦

Whether you turn to the right or to the left,
your ears will hear a voice behind you, saying,
"This is the way; walk in it."

—ISAIAH 30:21 (NIV)

This was not the way things were supposed to go.

Two years earlier, when we were a newly married couple, my husband, Brian, and I had moved from Colorado to northwest Arkansas. I quit my job as he relocated for his position, and we started our marriage in a fresh location, connecting into a growing church, and settling into a new home. It took a little while to adjust, but we were in a groove and things were falling into place.

And now this. Brian's company decided to get rid of an entire division and he was part of the layoff. What to do now?

Brian started reaching out to friends in his business world to see if they knew of any openings. I did the same thing, reaching out to old connections from my job in Colorado to see if that might be a possibility.

And we prayed.

We were a newly blended family with a teenager, and the idea of moving again to a whole new place didn't sit very well with her. Our daughter had a boy she liked, good friends, and played on a sports team. Moving was not on her radar. We prayed together, "Lord, direct us! Show us where you want us to be!"

During this time, I received a call from someone at the company I'd worked for in Colorado. My old position had opened back up. Would I be interested?

Could it be? While that seemed serendipitous, we just weren't sure. My husband's industry was based more in the Midwest; would he be able to find a good job if we moved back? While it would be great if I had a job, my income alone would not be enough to survive on, and they definitely would not pay to move us back to Colorado. It would be a big financial investment, especially if Brian wasn't able to find work there.

Lord, what do we do?

That evening we gathered around the TV to watch one of our favorite shows. It had been a tiring day of worry, frustration, and confusion. Brian was coming up empty with his colleagues and I was feeling overwhelmed by all that lay ahead. Uprooting and moving back to Colorado posed a lot of challenges, but we didn't seem to be getting any other leads or options, and time was running out.

Typically, we mute the commercials when we watch a show, but on this particular evening we were just too distracted to even think about it. We stared at the screen. Suddenly a mountain appeared, then some white-water rivers, then a beautiful sunset over Pikes Peak. The soothing voice of the ad announcer spilled over our hearts. "Colorful Colorado is the place for you!" At the same time, a slogan flashed across the screen. "Let's Talk Colorado."

Brian and I looked at each other. Our daughter looked at us. "No way," I said. "Why on earth is there a commercial for Colorado playing in northwest Arkansas?"

The next day I received an email from my old company, following up to see if I was interested in the job. That night the same commercial flashed on the screen. There was no denying it. God was absolutely telling us to move to Colorado and trust He would find a job opportunity for Brian.

Within a month, our home was packed up and we were driving back across the country to our new apartment in Colorado. I began working almost immediately at my old job while Brian kept scouring for opportunities that might be a good fit. He had been given three months of severance, and we had about thirty days' worth left. He found one position based in Minnesota. It seemed a long shot that they might allow him to work from Colorado, but with a prayer, he submitted his application.

Brian got the interview. He flew in for a second one. And by day eighty-eight of his severance, he received an offer. And yes, they were willing to let him be based in Colorado, because he would do sales throughout the country.

It was all just in time, just the way God planned. Just as He meant it to be.

Let's talk Colorado

You got it, Lord.

The Doubting Laundress

Pamela McMilian

—⧓————◦————⧓—

Teach me, LORD, the way of your decrees,
that I may follow it to the end.

—PSALM 119:33 (NIV)

What a glorious day! I thought as I drove. Sunshine warmed the car and the bright blue autumn sky over the road ahead held only a few cloud wisps. Glancing in the rearview mirror at the sleeping toddler in the back seat, my thoughts turned into prayers. *Thank You, Father, for another beautiful day. Thank You for all You do . . .*

My everyday prayers were interrupted by a sudden, specific prompting that was anything but ordinary: *Go to Sherry Taylor's home and ask to do her laundry.*

I was baffled.

What in the world was that? I wondered. *I don't even know Sherry. What would make me think of something like that?*

I knew who the Taylors were, of course. Everyone at church did. Sherry was a beautiful woman with dark curls and a movie-star smile. Her husband, Larry, was a large man with a fun personality and a great voice. He often took part in leading the worship services. The couple had several kids—maybe four or five. They usually sat near the front, filling a good portion of the row. But Sherry and I had never had a conversation. I doubted she even knew my name.

I tried to make sense of the startling thought, reasoning my way through it. *Maybe I just thought of her because I recently learned where they live and it's close by. But why would I think about her laundry? And it didn't seem like my own thought!*

Caught between doubt and a desire to obey, I returned to prayer.

Father, was that Your Spirit or just my imagination?

Nearing the Taylor home, with no immediate answer, I decided I didn't want to go home and always wonder if I should have stopped. There was only one way to know for sure.

Clasping my toddler's hand, I knocked on Sherry's front door and waited, listening for footsteps.

Instead, I thought I heard the faint call of a female voice. "Come in!"

Cracking the door slightly, I called out, "Hello? Sherry? Are you home?"

"Come on in!" came the reply.

Still clutching my little boy's hand and questioning my decision, I entered the home and closed the door behind me. *What are you doing?* I asked myself silently.

Sherry called out again. "I'm back here!"

I hesitated a moment and then walked tentatively down the long dim hallway toward the sound of her voice. The short-lived boldness I felt knocking on her door had not entered the house with me. *This is not a normal thing to do,* logic whispered.

"I'm in here," she called again as we neared the door of her dining room. The bright, sunlit room was now a makeshift bedroom. Sherry was sitting up in a bed with her left foot and ankle bandaged, taped, and propped on two fat pillows. Her wide-eyed expression indicated I wasn't who she expected to see in the doorway.

"Hi Sherry. I'm Pamela—from church." I introduced myself.

"Yes, yes, I recognize you," she smiled. "How are you?"

"I'm fine, but how are *you*?" I asked, pointing to her injured foot.

I felt the nudge in my spirit again.
Ask her about her laundry. *Taking a deep breath, I surrendered.*

"Oh, I was mowing. Barefoot." By the roll of her eyes, I knew she'd heard more than enough about shoes and mowing safety. She gave me an abbreviated version of her recent accident.

"I didn't see the glass bottle or whatever it was, in the yard and mowed over it. When the mower blade hit it, pieces of glass went flying. My foot was sliced up pretty badly. So I ended up in the emergency room with a bunch of stitches and antibiotics. Now I'm supposed to stay off my feet and keep this one elevated."

"Oh, Sherry, that's awful," I said. "Are you in much pain?"

"No, it's not too bad," she said. "It's getting better."

A moment of awkward silence made me aware that she must be wondering why I was there.

"Well, I don't want to interrupt your morning, I just took my daughter to school and thought I'd stop by on the way home and say hi. We'd better get going, but is there anything I can do for you?" I avoided the laundry question entirely, opting for a safer, general approach. "Do you need help with anything while you're healing up?"

"No, no." she said, dismissing the need for assistance with a wave of her hand. "Larry and the kids have been great and are taking care of everything for me."

My face felt warm. Awkwardness shifted to embarrassment. I hoisted my son to my hip. I wanted to prod further, but somehow couldn't make myself ask such a specific question.

"Are you sure?" I stalled. "Do you need anything from the store? I'd be happy to grocery shop or get whatever you need."

"No, we're all stocked up. Thank you, though."

I tried again.

"Is someone bringing meals for you? I'd be happy to bring supper over tonight."

"No, Larry does all the cooking. In fact, he's a great cook! And the kids are taking care of the house. We're fine. Really."

Getting nowhere with my questions and sensing I was on the cusp of overstaying I decided it was best to just leave before embarrassing myself further.

"Well, OK . . . I hope your foot heals up fast. If you need anything at all, just call. We're only a couple miles away," I said turning to go.

Stepping into the hallway, I felt a sinking disappointment in myself for not asking her about the laundry. *Why is this so hard?*

I felt the nudge in my spirit again. *Ask her about her laundry.* Taking a deep breath, I surrendered. Suddenly, embarrassing myself didn't matter.

"Sherry," I sighed, stepping back into the dining room. "I'm here because I keep feeling like I need to ask you about your laundry. Can I do your laundry for you?"

Sherry's eyes widened and filled with tears. Burying her face in her hands, she began to cry. Through tears, she explained that her washing machine had been broken for over a month.

I washed and praised God. I dried and praised God. I folded and praised God. Never have I experienced such a joyous laundry day!

"Larry hasn't had time to tend to the machine or even go to the laundromat. I can't go with my foot like this. He works all day and then comes home and takes care of me and the kids. I haven't wanted to bother him with it, but all that laundry piling up is really getting to me. I was praying about it just this morning."

"Well, I'm pretty sure the Lord wants me to take care of it for you," I said. The honesty felt good.

"Really?" she said, wiping tears with her hand. "There's a *lot*."

"Yes, really. That's why I'm here, Sherry. I felt like I was supposed to come to your house and ask if I could do your laundry. So just tell me where to find it and I'll take care of it."

Soon the car was filled with laundry baskets and my little one and I were heading home. The excitement of the morning's experience fueled my day. I washed and praised God. I dried and praised God. I folded and praised God. Never have I experienced such a joyous laundry day!

It was hard to say whose heart was more grateful that evening when I returned to Sherry's with the baskets of clean clothes. We each marveled at how good God is, and how He cares about all the details of our lives. He had heard and answered her morning prayer. And I had learned to recognize His voice more clearly and the important lesson of overcoming doubt through surrender.

God's Mysterious Ways: Putting Aside Embarrassment

Sometimes God asks us to do things that are difficult—like doing someone else's laundry. But what a great blessing that can be to the other person! Jesus said if we want to be great in God's kingdom, we need to be a servant to all (Mark 9:35), no matter how humbling that experience might be. Or maybe even for that very reason!

- **Pray.** Pray for God to give you opportunities to serve others, even if the task feels awkward or embarrassing. And then pray that when you need help, you will receive it with grace as a gift from God.

- **Seek.** Be proactive. There's always someone who needs a hand, whether it's a meal, housecleaning, help with laundry, or even free childcare for a tired mama. Look for ways to serve others.

- **Act.** The apostle James said it doesn't do anyone any good just to say, "Be warmed and be filled," and then not give them what they need. If God prompts you to fill a need in someone's life, do it. You will receive from God what you have given up and more.

- **Reflect.** When have you seen this principle be true? Has anyone served you humbly and graciously in the past? How hard is it for you to receive such help? How can you make the offer of this humble help from others easier by your response?

When a Blessing Needs Project Management

Rhoda Blecker

You need fear misfortune no more.

—Zephaniah 3:15 (JPS)

I have always disliked the whole idea of surgery. When friends need it, that's one thing. But if someone says I need it, I just about run for the hills. So when my nurse practitioner suggested I have some plastic surgery we all considered "discretionary," at first I refused. "If it's dependent on my discretion, the answer will always be 'no,'" I said.

But she kept after me, and my husband, Keith, agreed with her after she insisted that my back would turn into a corkscrew if I didn't have a mammoplasty.

In the spring of 2000, I finally gave in and scheduled the surgery for March 2001. But in January 2001, the hospital notified me that necessary surgeries had crowded their schedule, and they would need to postpone all their discretionary surgeries to other dates. Mine had been rescheduled to July. I was delighted. That meant I could relax, since, as I described it to Keith, they would not be "carving me up" until later. Secretly, I was just hoping they would cancel it altogether.

Never mind what might happen to my back—my skin could remain unbroken, which meant to me that my spirit would remain unbroken as well.

I tried to put the thought of being sliced and diced aside and lived day to day in the thickets of routine. Nevertheless, thoughts of another time I'd been in a hospital kept intruding. When I was fourteen years old, I had my wisdom teeth removed. As a child who had been molested by a medical professional starting at age nine, I was already leery of times when someone else had control over me—and someone in a position of medical power was especially terrifying. So when the anesthetist for the dental surgery told me that as soon as I was unconscious, he was going to make love to me, I blew my stack and created havoc in the operating room. That experience was the reason for my deep reluctance to subject myself to anesthesia another time, no matter how good the purpose.

As July approached, I became more and more uneasy, but before things could get too bad, the hospital rescheduled my surgery for November. I relaxed immediately. Keith was very aware of the change in me, the relief, the return of humor. He didn't say anything, but I could tell it was easier for him to live with me when an operation was not dominating my thoughts.

By November, my surgery had been postponed yet again, this time to April 2002. I began to hope that it would never happen, but inevitably, time began to tick down again. I was delighted when it was moved one more time, to Friday, July 19. Something told me they were not going to postpone it any longer—they had been bumping me for a solid year, and I doubted they would keep it up longer than that. The sense of inevitability increased my anxiety as the day came closer.

I began to jump at loud noises, toss and turn instead of sleep, and either had no appetite or would eat a lot of things calculated to be bad for me. Keith kept trying to tell me everything would be OK, but the fear was stronger than his reassurances.

At the end of May, I got an invitation to attend a Guideposts dinner at a booksellers conference being held within driving distance of our home. The conference had not been in Southern California for years. Keith and I normally would have passed on it because it was on a weekday and the traffic would be bad; it could take us three hours to get there. But the dinner was scheduled for the week before my looming operation. Both of us thought it would be a distraction for me, so we agreed to go.

The dinner was scheduled for the week before my looming operation. My husband and I thought it would be a distraction for me, so we agreed to go.

At that point, I had been writing for Guideposts' devotional *Daily Guideposts* (now called *Walking in Grace*) for several years. I was accustomed to turning in devotions well in advance of publication, and I never know on which dates they would appear in a volume; the editors placed them throughout the year, depending on where the devotions fit best.

Because I would be seeing other Guideposts authors and meeting editors, I thought I should probably look at the most recent *Daily Guideposts* to remind myself what I had written and to memorize other names, because I might meet someone else with contributions to the book. I couldn't find my copy, though. There were other years of the series in the bookcases, in the "to be read" pile on my desk, and on the floor of my office, but the one I needed was nowhere to be found. I kept searching for it right up to the date of the dinner, with no success.

The day we drove south to the conference venue, I had resigned myself to looking ignorant. I couldn't even remember what I had written for the volume. I comforted myself by thinking that if I couldn't remember it, likely no one else could, either.

The room where the authors' dinner was being held had been set up with a number of round, eight-person tables, but what caught my attention instantly was each centerpiece. It consisted of a circle of eight copies of that year's *Daily Guideposts*. A lovely gesture—and very fortuitous, because I would be able to replace the one I couldn't find. I had no idea just how good the timing would be.

The dinner was fun and tasty. It also served the purpose of distracting me with pleasant company and good conversation, so that the persistent fear of—as I saw it—my imminent butchery was effectively muted. It was very late and fully dark out when we were able to break up the centerpieces with our copies of *Daily Guideposts*, say goodnight to new friends, and hit the freeways to go home.

The next morning, I remembered that I could finally see what devotionals I had written for the year. I looked up my name in the index, and listed next to it was a series called "A Grand Canyon Journey." What? I had never intentionally written a series.

Wondering what I had written to inspire the editors to assign all my devotions to one set of dates, I turned to first page. I'd written about rafting the Colorado River, a marvelous and spirit-filled trip I'd done ten times by then. I started smiling, turned to look at the first devotion—then gasped and sat down hard.

Day one of the series had been placed on Saturday, July 20. The devotion began with the words, "My journey into the Grand Canyon began, improbably enough, in a hospital bed in Los Angeles."

I began to shake. The devotion told the story of the last time I'd had surgery and how I had emerged from it into one of the greatest experiences of my life. And the entire series had somehow been scheduled to begin the morning after my upcoming surgery and continue into the week of my recovery.

The devotion began with the words, "My journey into the Grand Canyon began, improbably enough, in a hospital bed in Los Angeles."

As I sat unmoving with the book in my hands, I started thinking about everything that had come together to bring me to this particular revelation: I had to have written my devotions about the Canyon trip without any knowledge that I would need their reassurance later. The editors at Guideposts had to have decided to put them together, and picked the dates they would occupy in the book. The booksellers' association had to have picked Southern California for their meeting that year. And the hospital had to keep postponing my surgery until it fit neatly into all the other factors—all so that I could understand how my present fears were unnecessary and probably silly.

I called out to Keith and babbled out the entire story, ending it by saying, "God had to work really hard on a whole lot of people to pull this one off!"

"God's obviously a great project manager," Keith replied. "You'd better pay attention."

Acknowledgments

Every attempt has been made to credit the sources of copyrighted material used in this book. If any such acknowledgment has been inadvertently omitted or miscredited, receipt of such information would be appreciated.

Scripture quotations marked (ESV) are taken from *The Holy Bible, English Standard Version*. Copyright © 2001 by Crossway Bibles, a division of Good News Publishers. Used by permission. All rights reserved.

Scripture quotations marked (JPS) are taken from *Tanakh: A New Translation of the Holy Scriptures according to the Traditional Hebrew Text*. Copyright © 1985 by the Jewish Publication Society. All rights reserved.

Scripture quotations marked (KJV) are taken from the *King James Version of the Bible*.

Scripture quotations marked (NIV) are taken from *The Holy Bible, New International Version*®, *NIV*®. Copyright © 1973, 1978, 1984, 2011 by Biblica, Inc. Used by permission. All rights reserved worldwide.

Scripture quotations marked (NKJV) are taken from the *New King James Version*®. Copyright © 1982 by Thomas Nelson. Used by permission. All rights reserved.

Scripture quotations marked (NLT) are taken from the *Holy Bible, New Living Translation*. Copyright © 1996, 2004, 2007, 2015 by Tyndale House Foundation. Used by permission of Tyndale House Publishers Inc., Carol Stream, Illinois. All rights reserved.

Scripture quotations marked (RSV) are taken from the *Revised Standard Version of the Bible*. Copyright © 1946, 1952, 1971 by the Division of Christian Education of the National Council of the Churches of Christ in the United States of America. Used by permission.

A Note from the Editors

We hope you enjoyed *Guided by His Hand,* published by Guideposts. For more than seventy-five years, Guideposts, a nonprofit organization, has been driven by a vision of a world filled with hope. We aspire to be the voice of a trusted friend, a friend who makes you feel more hopeful and connected.

By making a purchase from Guideposts, you join our community in touching millions of lives, inspiring them to believe that all things are possible through faith, hope, and prayer. Your continued support allows us to provide uplifting resources to those in need. Whether through our communities, websites, apps, or publications, we inspire our audiences, bring them together, and comfort, uplift, entertain, and guide them. Visit us at guideposts.org to learn more.

We would love to hear from you. Write us at Guideposts, P.O. Box 5815, Harlan, Iowa 51593 or call us at (800) 932-2145. Did you love *Guided by His Hand?* Leave a review for this product on guideposts.org/shop. Your feedback helps others in our community find relevant products.

Find inspiration, find faith, find Guideposts.

Shop our best sellers and favorites at
guideposts.org/shop

Or scan the QR code to go directly to our Shop